The Multi-Camera Director

Edition 2 - July, 1998
ISBN 9647401-2-5
Printed in the United States of America

Western Media Products
P.O. Box 591
Denver, Colorado 80201

ABOUT THE AUTHOR

Mark Herlinger holds a B.A. in radio-TV-film from the University of Michigan and an M.A. in journalism from the University of Colorado. Since 1981, he has directed documentaries, public affairs programs, talk shows, educational and entertainment programs. He has received regional emmy awards for directing, and his performing arts productions have been broadcast nationally by PBS. Since 1986, he has taught TV production at the University of Colorado, Boulder and Denver campuses, and at Metropolitan State College of Denver. Currently, Mark Herlinger is an independent producer/director, instructor, and author in Denver.

OTHER TITLES

The Single-Camera Director
Directing Major Market TV News (video)
The Multi-Camera Director Supplement

ACKNOWLEDGMENTS

The author acknowledges the influences of professors: Edward Stasheff, Garnett Garrison, Henry Austin, and Edgar Willis—former faculty members of the University of Michigan Television Department.

Special thanks to the following people for technical assistance:
Professor Emeritus Edward Stasheff, University of Michigan; Professor Steve Jones, Assistant Dean, School of Journalism and Mass Communications, University of Colorado; Paul and Ilona Herlinger, Jodie Haselton, Peter Ziskin

Design & production: A. B. Forster
Copy editing: Teresa Herlinger
Additional production: Janet Roucis

The following companies generously donated commercials and PSAs for the Multi-Camera Director Media Kit:
American Heart Association
Boeing Company
Ford Motor Company
Hart Media Group
J. Walter Thompson Company
KDVR 31
Mother's Against Drunk Driving
Peace Corps

CONTENTS

The Multi-Camera Director

INTRODUCTION

A one-hour studio-based TV variety show is about to be broadcast live across the country.

"5,4,3,2..." the assistant director counts down to the start of the program.

"Cue talent, Fade 1," calls the director. As the switcher and floor manager each respond to their respective commands, camera ① comes on line and the host begins to speak.

The show is live—the signal is instantly fed to a transmitter and everything that happens, good or bad, will be seen by millions of viewers.

If that isn't exciting enough, consider the fact that this program is using five cameras, seven VTR roll-ins, eight commercial breaks, ten live announcements, three set changes, four guest changes, and a music number by an eight-piece jazz band.

The TV director is both choreographer and conductor of this complex undertaking and hopes that all the rehearsing will pay off during the course of the next hour. For now, at seconds past the 8:00 P.M. airtime, the director and crew are executing their first and final performance.

Directing a multi-camera TV production is an entirely different experience from directing the single-camera, film-style production in which material is shot with one camera and edited later. The skills required to make all things flow together harmoniously in real time makes a studio-based multi-camera TV production a singular experience, guaranteed to raise your heart rate—at least for the duration of the program!

For any student considering a career in TV production, it's helpful to experience the pace of live-style multi-camera production while in school.

That experience can be had in the classroom or through internships with TV stations—especially those stations that do daily live newscasts. Some students will discover that the fast pace of a multi-camera production is exactly what they like. Others may choose film-style production as a preferable pace at which to work.

This book, when used in a classroom context with fellow students as crew, will allow you to get some of that experience—a preview of what multi-camera production is all about. It will guide you through the fundamentals of live directing as well as the skills needed to perform crew positions.

The information here should also stimulate your ideas. Those ideas, coupled with the skills developed, can become the tools wielded by a thoughtful, creative director toward the production of a well-crafted television program. Therein lies the academic component of this process—it isn't just about learning how to push buttons and roll videotape machines. Rather, it's about learning to communicate a message within the parameters of a particular form—live television. What you bring to the studio with your own educational background will influence the quality of your production and the compelling nature of your message.

TV production taught in the academic environment should combine the broad-based knowledge of a good liberal arts education with the skills required to direct a TV production. The more knowledge you bring to the studio—good use of language, awareness of current events, history, art, etc. together with the directing skills you'll learn from a book like this, the more power you will have to craft a program with intellectual and artistic integrity.

For example, the TV director is constantly dealing with word choice and grammar. The ability to catch an error in a script, or to tactfully correct a host who uses a word incorrectly, is a valuable asset that a director can bring to his or her production.

Not everyone in a TV crew is saddled with this responsibility. But the director should be. He or she is both leader and visionary for the entire production. People will look to the director for answers to all kinds of questions.

Producer and Director

In the professional world of television and film, there is another authority on hand as well—the producer of the program. People often wonder what the difference is between the producer and director. Part of the answer is simple: the producer has authority over the director and therefore has an even greater responsibility for questions and problems relating to the production.

The more complicated part of the answer is that the producer's and director's areas of authority often overlap. You may encounter different balances of power between a producer and a director from situation to situation. In some cases, the producer will give the director specific guidelines about the artistic execution of the program. In other cases, the director will have a great deal of leeway to make his or her own judgment calls.

In general, the producer is responsible for the overall concept of the show as well as logistical and financial concerns. The director is responsible for the actual execution of the production. In each working relationship, the terms of authority and responsibility between producer and director should be agreed upon at the outset of the project.

In TV news, for example, the producer is in charge of the newscast. He or she decides on the stories and the overall structure of the program. The producer will add or cut stories throughout the day as certain stories take priority. If breaking news happens during a newscast and the story sequence suddenly needs to be changed, the producer decides on the changes and the director carries them out. In short, the producer is responsible for story content and the director is responsible for technical execution. In order for the newscast to run well, the producer and director need to be in close communication throughout the day. During the newscast, they usually sit close to one another for easy communication.

So how is the role of a TV director best expressed? The director's most distinguishing quality is that he or she must be, above all, the liaison between the technical and conceptual worlds. The TV business is like no other in its attempt to marry these two vastly dissimilar worlds. The conceptual side includes producers, writers, performers, artists. The technical side includes engineers and technicians. Nobody is more responsible for understanding both worlds and acting as the diplomat to bring them both together than the director. A good director will speak both languages.

In summary, the TV director is much more than a technician. The director is also a leader, a problem-solver, a communicator, and an artist.

USING THIS BOOK

The lessons and exercises in this workbook are designed to complement the studio directing portion of any beginning or intermediate TV production class.

Today, most college level TV production classes are associated with journalism or mass communication departments. That's why the exercises in this book focus on news and public affairs. However, fundamental skills that are developed in this workbook apply to any type of multi-camera production, including sports and entertainment.

Part I of this book prepares the student for multi-camera directing. These chapters cover specific skill-related topics such as script-marking, segment timing, and crew positions.

In Part II, you'll find a series of thirteen scripts to be used as in-studio performance exercises, involving the rest of the class as crew, but emphasizing the role of the director. Each script is preceded by an orientation to the new factors appearing in that script.

Some of these exercises are in the form of newscasts. Others are demonstration-style, interview-style, and variety show formats.

Studio facility requirements for these script exercises include: two studio cameras, switcher, lighting, microphones, character generator, audiotape playback, VTR playback, and VTR recording.

Class instructors have available to them a media kit that accompanies this workbook containing materials for each script exercise. The kit includes:

1. Easel graphics: foam-core mounted photos and graphics for cameras to frame in the studio.

2. Videotape segments such as: commercials, news stories, features, opening title segments, and closing title segments.

3. Music themes, each exactly one minute long.

Instructors may use as many or as few of the exercises as they desire. Instructors may also choose to modify any of these script exercises. For example, the class might produce a videotape roll-in for a given exercise instead of using the one provided. Or, the script may have to be modified to suit the available technical facilities of your studio.

Another option is to use any of the thirteen scripts as in-class exercises instead of in-studio productions, allowing students to simply study and review such skills as script-marking and segment timing.

For all scripts that actually get produced in the studio, the premise is that each member of the class will have the opportunity to direct each script selected by the instructor. The class rotates through all the crew positions, each student taking his or her turn to direct the same exercise.

If an exercise is too simple for the class, the instructor may opt to skip ahead to one that is more challenging. However, before skipping on to a more difficult exercise, there is an important consideration that affects the difficulty rating of an exercise: the amount of rehearsal time allotted.

For example, twenty minutes per rotation gives each student director about fifteen minutes to get prepared and rehearse before his or her designated air time, at which point the actual show gets taped. In some cases, twenty minutes will seem more than adequate; in complex exercises, twenty minutes may present a challenge or seem insufficient.

This workbook does not prescribe the amount of rehearsal time for any of the exercises. Instructors can vary the class rotation intervals in order to lighten or heighten the pressure to prepare quickly and efficiently. As the learning curve accelerates, the instructor may shorten rehearsal time to increase the challenge.

Student production in progress

Some instructors build a "bye" into the rotation schedule, giving each student a chance to sit out one rotation to observe the process and prepare mentally before sitting in the director's hot seat.

When short on crew, double-up. Here, the Floor Manager doubles as Announcer.

Class Size

Since class sizes will vary, the instructor may modify the crew. For example, if the class is too small, a floor assistant may double as a studio announcer. On the other hand, if a class is large, the instructor might create extra positions such as additional floor assistants. Or the instructor may create an additional "bye" so that a director can sit out for two rotations prior to his or her turn. This workbook relies on the instructor to adapt these exercises to available technical facilities and class size.

Two Cameras

All thirteen script exercises in this book are designed to be used with two cameras. In many studios, there may only be two cameras anyway. But even if the studio has three or more cameras available, it is recommended that students demonstrate a high level of competence using two cameras before adding a third.

One major directing challenge is the planning of camera shots. How will the director cover many shots with a few cameras? The director must choreograph a flow of movement that allows one camera to prepare the upcoming shot while the other camera is "on-the-air" or "hot" on the current shot.

On one hand, having many cameras makes the director's job easier. There is less problem distributing the shot sequence among the camera operators. On the other hand, three or more cameras mean more to keep track of—more potential for confusion.

The director constantly faces logistical challenges: quickly sending cameras to different parts of the studio in time for upcoming shots, or changing framing from talent to easel and back in just a few seconds. The initial use of two cameras requires the student to carefully consider how to orchestrate these camera changes. By learning and practicing with two cameras, a student can develop a fast and efficient method. This skill will pay off in later complex situations. Then, when the student director has demonstrated efficient use of two cameras, it may be time to add a third.

Two-camera production: a one-on-one interview.

Pre-opening of WPIX-TV, New York, 1948.

CONCEPTS BEHIND MULTI-CAMERA DIRECTING

Broadcast television dates back to 1939 with coverage of the opening of the New York World's Fair. Until videotape came along seventeen years later (1956), television was live—except for a rather poor resolution film recording process known as "kinescope" which involved aiming a film camera at a TV monitor.

For broadcast TV production, there was no luxury of shooting first on videotape and editing later. Every aspect of the TV production had to be planned and rehearsed before being executed in real time. Any transitions—cuts, dissolves, and wipes—had to be done using a switcher in a multi-camera situation, either in a TV studio, or on a live remote truck containing a TV control room.

Consequently, the TV director had little choice but to be proficient at multi-camera directing. That style defined the TV director and made the job quite different from film directing.

Multi-camera or single-camera

Even though much of modern day TV is edited, there is still a constant need for multi-camera directing skills. Many types of programs—sports events, news coverage, talk shows—must be televised using multi-camera techniques.

By contrast, film-style, also called single-camera, directing involves shooting with one camera. The sequence of shots and angles cannot be filmed in real time. Instead, the talent might repeat dialogue in order to accommodate the need to move the camera around for individual close-up shots and reverse-angle shots. Each shot, each angle, can be dealt with carefully and slowly, one at a time, both in the shooting process and later in the editing process.

Today, a TV director may choose either style: film-style, using a single camera and editing later, or live style, where everything happens simultaneously. Both styles are often used within a single program. Most news, talk shows, and special events are done live but may contain pre-packaged film-style segments.

Thus, live-style directing is by no means a thing of the past. Anyone who wishes to have diverse skills in TV directing, or who expects to work on multi-camera productions such as news, sports, talk shows, or live events, will be much better prepared by having mastered the basic skills described in this workbook.

Studio or remote

A multi-camera program may be produced in a studio or on location such as a theater or sports arena. Unlike the single-camera method of taking one camera in the field, multi-camera remote production requires taking a large amount of gear on location: cameras, switchers, test equipment, videotape machines, audio boards, and more.

In most cases, remote productions employ a large truck with a built-in control room. That way, all the support equipment stays together and can be easily transported. Once you see how much equipment is required in the field for a remote multi-camera production, you can appreciate the ease of keeping it all safely at home in a studio.

Live or live-to-tape

A program may be recorded on tape first, but directed as if it were live. This is called *live-to-tape*. There are several reasons why this often occurs in the TV industry:

1. A program may be taped for delayed broadcast, e.g. 7P.M. EST taped for broadcast at 7P.M. MST, two hours later.

2. Time constraints. The air date may be a day away. No time to shoot the show single-camera style and edit the entire program. The show must be done live-to-tape in order to be ready soon enough. Perhaps a small amount of editing will be needed for opening/closing titles, or to fix a major mistake.

Multi-camera production. The director coordinates the simultaneous action of two or more cameras in a studio.

Single-camera film-style production. One camera is used to record all images for eventual editing.

3 It may be illogical to do the show any other but than live-style. The taping of a talk show, for example, which needs instant cutting back and forth, would be impractical to shoot single-camera style. A conversation between two or more people has a natural flow when captured in a live or live-to-tape fashion using two or more cameras.

Live-to-tape provides a legitimate live directing experience. Even if these exercises are not actually broadcast live, students can still have a live experience by recording live-to-tape—students adhere to air times as if they were directing live productions. Instructors can record class exercises on tape, then play back the finished work for review in class.

Air times

A live program usually has a specific air time. The biggest challenge in live multi-camera directing is to be ready by that prescribed air time.

At a TV news station, the news may be broadcast several times a day, for example: 5:00pm and 10:00pm. Each day, the director must backtime his or her preparation in order to be ready on time. Early in the day, the director will meet with the news director and news producers to go over the rundown of segments and stories for each of the evening broadcasts.

The director then spends several hours going over scripts and rundowns, making a myriad of decisions: Which camera will be on the talent for any given segment? Which VTR will be used to play back a given videotape news package from a field reporter? Which segments require additional titles or graphics to be generated from the control room? The director marks the script with commands that he or she will call out to the crew during the newscast in order to initiate all these decisions at the right time. When the show starts, it's too late to start making these decisions. The director should already have played out the newscast in his or her mind, imaging what will need to happen every moment along the way. Then, as the airtime draws near, the director and crew gather in the control room and go over last minute details so that everyone is ready for the air time.

A director who cannot be ready on time won't last very long on the job. Thus, learning to deal effectively with impending air times is the most valuable thing a student can do to prepare for the professional world. To facilitate this practice, instructors can assign air times for each exercise. Adhering to the prescribed air time with absolutely no excuses or exceptions is a great way to learn the discipline of live directing.

The total block of time in class allotted to each student for executing a production should include a modest but adequate amount of rehearsal time. The rehearsal must be brought to an end in time for the imminent air time. Once the show is over, the class rotates and repeats the process with the next director. For example, a student may be assigned a rehearsal beginning at 2:45 P.M. followed by an air time of 3:00 P.M. When the five-minute program ends at 3:05 P.M., the class rotates and the next director has a turn.

CREW POSITIONS

While the student on the left directs, the other students act as crew. The student to the right is operating the video switcher.

The focus of most studio-based production courses is on the director. However, the crew is vitally important to any production. Learning crew positions is just as important as learning how to direct. In fact, the best directors are those that have had experience in various crew positions and understand the required skills.

The crew can make the director look good or bad. A camera operator, for example, who can't focus or hold a steady shot will compromise a nicely conceived program—and will no doubt upset a director who has spent time preparing.

The Golden Rule applies: Try to be a good crew person for your fellow classmates when they direct, just as you will most certainly want them to be a good crew for you when you direct.

Naturally, mistakes will be made in a learning situation. Everyone will have their share of faux pas. But in a situation where everyone works together so intimately, the class will quickly discern who is trying to master the skills of each crew position and who is not putting in much effort.

The following pages offer a summary of crew positions and required skills. Notice the typical abbreviation associated with each position. These shorthand notations will be used throughout the book.

Director and assistant director (AD) sit in the control room, monitoring cameras located in the neighboring studio.

Keep in mind that most multi-camera facilities include both a studio and a separate control room. Some crew members are stationed in the control room, others are in the studio.

CREW POSITIONS

Director - DIR

DIR is a shorthand symbol for director. The DIR sits in the control room and calls the shots for the live or live-to-tape show. Since some crew members may in other places out of hearing range, the crew members all wear intercom headsets to hear the director's cues.

Assistant Director - AD

The AD sits next to the DIR in the control room and provides general support. Typically, that support includes:

- Keeping track of time. The AD keeps the DIR apprised of time remaining in the rehearsal period, time remaining until air time, and time remaining during each segment of the show. The DIR could do all this if he or she had no choice. But the AD takes a load of responsibility off the DIR's shoulders by keeping track of time.
- The AD may also assist by communicating with crew members to make sure that everything is ready as needed: crew in position, videotapes loaded for play back, titles and graphics ready, etc.
- The AD may also watch monitors to double check for shot accuracy and shot composition.
- Finally, the AD is at the DIR's general disposal. The DIR may inform the AD of any additional responsibilities.

Floor Manager - FM

(sometimes called Floor Director)
The FM is the DIR's voice and hands in the studio. Communicating by intercom, the DIR relays commands via the FM. The talent—hosts, anchors, etc.—look to the FM for start cues to begin speaking or to start action. The FM also keeps order in the studio and makes sure everything is ready to go.

The Floor Manager stands near the talent's camera and gives cues and signals for the director.

Most often, the FM silently cues talent to begin. Cuing the talent should be a very clear throw of a pointed finger directly at the talent. The Floor Manager first keeps a hand raised in the air to signify ready and stand by, then a quick point to the talent for the actual cue to begin when the director calls the command.

Here are some signals given by the FM to the talent in order to maintain silence while a show is in progress:

The Floor Manager should stand as close to the talent's camera as possible and up front by the lens when giving any signals or time cues to the talent. By doing so, the talent can notice the signals while addressing the camera without appearing to be distracted.

Time cues - Time cues may be given with hand signals or by holding up cards which indicate: 5 min. remaining, 4 min. remaining, etc.

Stretch - Pulling hands apart as if spreading taffy means, "Take a little extra time with your delivery."

Speed up - Making a quick circular motion with a pointed finger signifies the need for the talent to speed up.

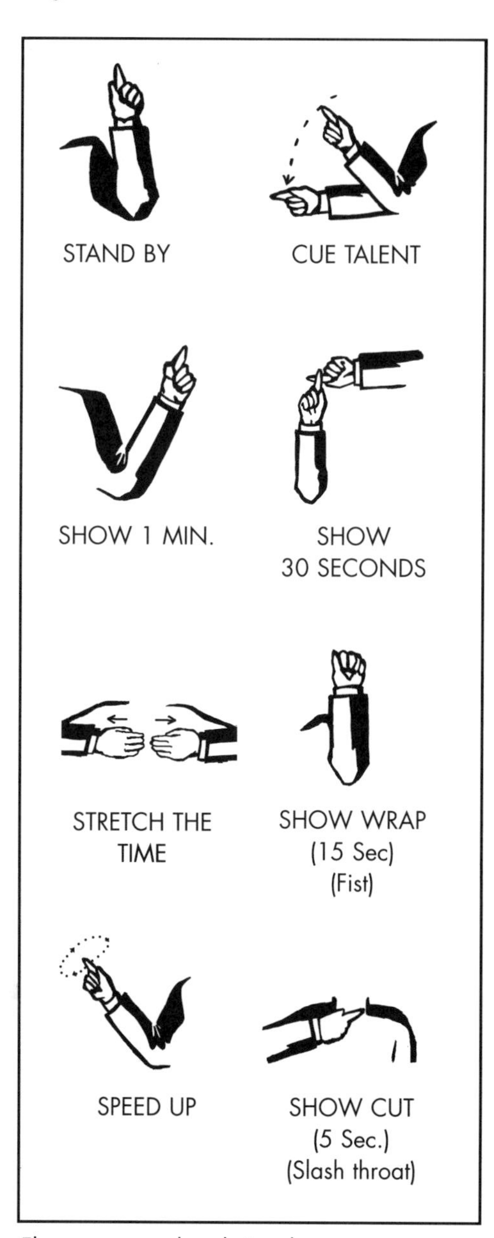

Floor manager hand signals.

Camera operators for cameras 1 & 2. Each operator wears a headset to hear the director's instructions for framing, panning, tilting, trucking, dollying, and breaking to different shots.

Camera Operator - CAM

The camera operator is expected to execute smooth and clean camera moves and to frame shots with an eye for good composition. The director will ask camera operators for specific moves or shot changes through the intercom system such as, "zoom in," "pan right," "frame up the easel graphic," etc.

Review of camera moves

A *pan* is a side to side move. You pan left or pan right. When the DIR calls "pan left," the camera operator should move the tripod handle to the right which makes the lens move left. This is often confusing for the novice and may take a little bit of getting used to.

A *tilt* is an up and down move. You tilt up or tilt down. When the DIR calls "tilt up," the camera operator moves the tripod handle down so that the lens moves up.

A *zoom* is a modern day convenience. In the past, a camera came with a turret of fixed focal length lenses. The operator would dial in a telephoto lens or a wide angle lens. Today, the zoom enables the operator to quickly prepare a change of framing from wide angle to telephoto by simply pushing a motor control button on the lens. The camera operator can zoom in or zoom out. Most zoom lenses have servo motor controls which means that the softer you push the button, the slower the zoom.

A *dolly* is a physical move of the camera toward the subject or away from the subject. You dolly in or dolly out. A dolly requires wheels on the base of the tripod. It's important to align the wheels ahead of time so that the operator can push or pull the camera in a straight line without extraneous wobbles. A floor assistant can help prepare the move by setting the wheels in the right direction.

A *truck* is a physical move of the camera from side to side. You can truck left or truck right. Again, wheels are necessary.

An *arc* is also a side to side move but with a bit of an arc to it. You may wish to move the camera around an object and maintain a constant radius from the subject, so you arc instead of truck.

Focusing

To understand focusing a camera lens, you have to understand the term *depth of field*. For any given focus setting, there is a point out in front of your lens that is in focus. We call that the *focal point*. The distance in front of and behind the focal point that is also in sharp focus is called the depth of field. Depth of field may vary depending on the focal length of the lens.

Physics says that the more telephoto your lens is (zoomed in), the less depth of field. The wider your lens angle (zoomed out), the greater the depth of field. Let's imagine that your subject is a news anchor behind a desk. Your field of view is wide. You might have a depth of field that extends three feet in front of and behind the subject. The subject appears to be in focus simply because he falls within the depth of field. However, as you zoom in, the lens becomes more telephoto and the depth of field diminishes rapidly. As you zoom in, you discover that your focal point was not actually on the talent, but rather a few inches behind him. Alas, his face begins to go soft as you zoom to a close-up because the depth of field has shrunk around the true focal point.

The only way to have avoided that embarrassment would have been to zoom all the way in and focus on the talent's face before going on line. By doing so, you would have determined your focal point with the worst possible depth of field.

So the rule is: To prepare, always zoom in as far as possible on your subject in order to set focus.

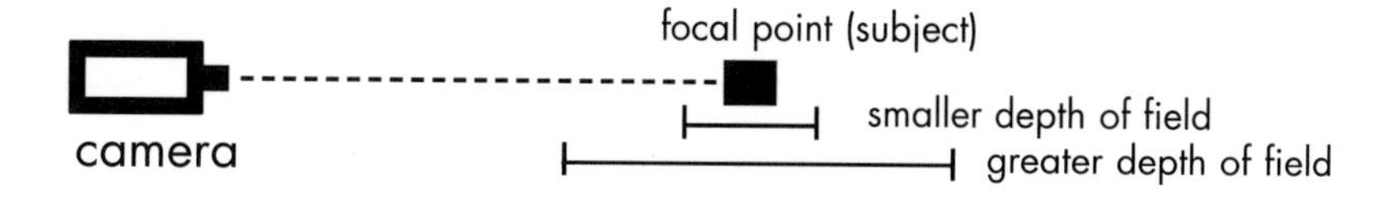

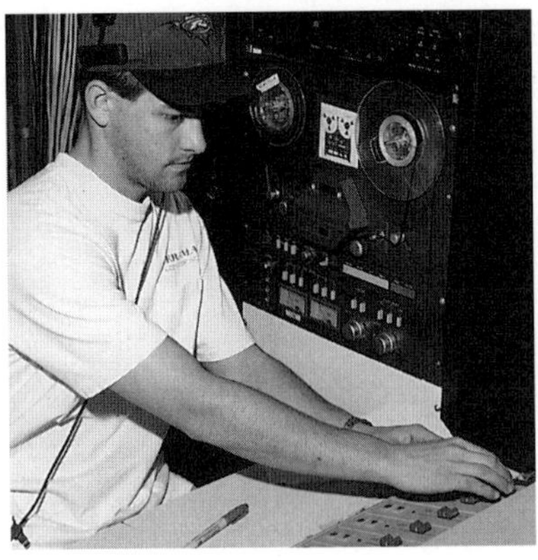

Audio engineer

AUD controls the recording volume of all microphones and tape machines with the Audio Mixer

Audio - AUD

The audio engineer is usually stationed in the control room near the director or in a nearby sound booth. This crew person places microphones in the studio and operates the audio mixer through which all audio sources pass: mics, audio tapes, VTR audio, record player, CD player, etc. The AUD person should be able to:

- carry out audio commands and cues
- operate audio mixer
- operate audio playback machines
- slip cue records if records are used
- understand audio transitions: sneaks, fades, hits
- choose appropriate microphones
- set mics in the studio
- understand the VU meter in order to set proper audio levels

The audio engineer may have an assistant, known as Audio 2 or A2. The assistant usually stays in the studio for mic placement while the main audio person—called A1— sits in the control room at the mixer.

An audio engineer should be aware of the types of microphones that are available for your use. Which will you choose? Sometimes it is helpful to include audio design and layout in the floor plan or to make a separate audio scheme on paper for the audio engineer if the placement of microphones becomes complex.

Microphones are classified by three factors:

1. style (hand-held, lavaliere, boom)
2. power source (battery or other power supply needed?)
3. pickup pattern (unidirectional, omni-directional, cardioid)

For example, your best microphone choice for a host sitting in a chair might be a lavaliere that has a cardioid pattern and requires 48 volt *phantom power* from a battery pack. Or, your best mic choice for a dramatic scene might be a boom mic using a shotgun that has a hypercardioid pattern and requires a 9.3 volt battery.

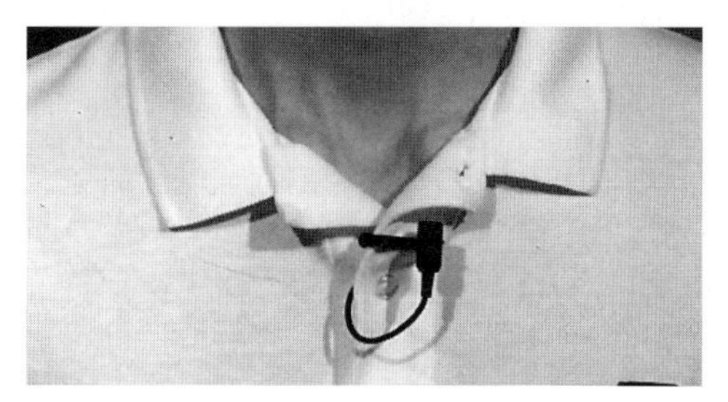

Style: lavaliere or clip-on
Use: interviews or spokespeople
Advantage: Close and fairly inconspicuous
Pick-up pattern: omni-directional
Power requirement: battery

Style: hand-held
Use: interviews or stand-up reporters.
Advantage: Can be held close to the mouth
Pick-up pattern: cardioid
Power requirement: none

Style: shotgun
Use: dramatic scenes, on-the-run news and documentary
Advantage: Works well at a slight distance. Can be held just out of the frame so as not to be seen
Pick-up pattern: super-cardioid
Power requirement: battery

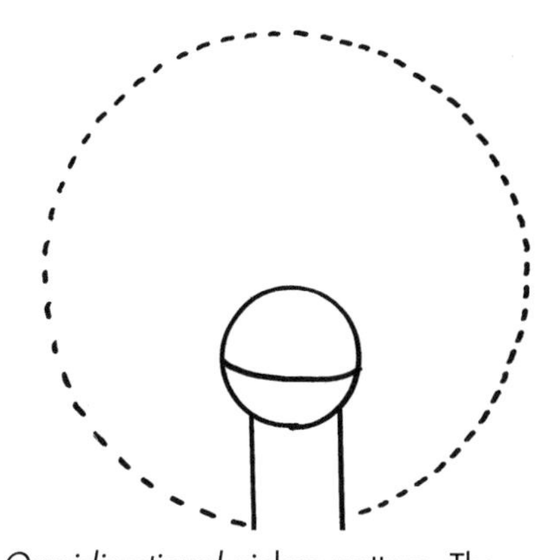

Omnidirectional pickup pattern. The mic senses sound equally in a complete sphere. You might use this for a music ensemble.

Unidirectional pickup pattern. The mic is only sensitive directly in front. This is good when you don't want nearby sounds to be heard. A singer in a band may use one.

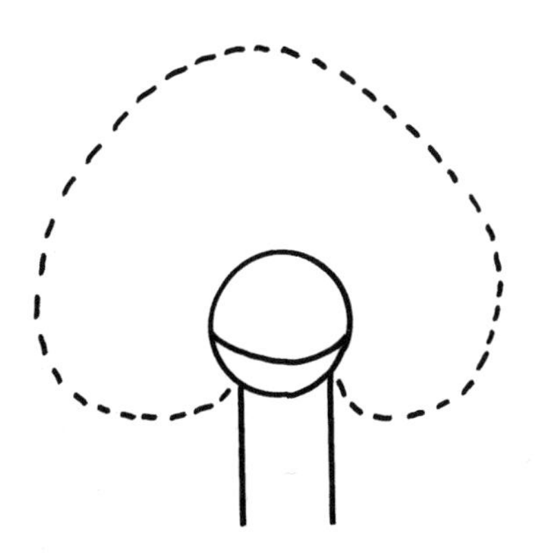

Cardioid pickup pattern. The sensitivity range is a little bit broader than a unidirectional mic. Good for stand-up reporters and talk show hosts

Technical Director - TD (Also called "switcher")
The *switcher* is both a piece of equipment and the person who operates it. That person may be called the switcher or the technical director or TD. He or she sits in the control room, next to the DIR.

The TD should:
- understand the functions of the switcher
- be proficient at cuts, fades, wipes, dissolves, and keys

The TD or switcher operates a large board full of buttons also called a switcher. This board of buttons integrates all video sources similar to the way an audio board integrates all audio sources.

The TD may select among video sources such as: cameras 1 and 2, character generator (CG) for word graphics, VTR for video playback, any color for a color background, or video black for a black screen to fade up from and down to before and after each program.

The TD uses fader bar on the switcher to perform a dissolve or wipe.

Sources such as cameras, VTRs, and character generators are selected with buttons on the switcher. Black is a source as well. Fading to or from black requires this source.

The Technical Director, also called the "switcher," sits at the video switcher console and performs all video transitions as the director calls them.

Why is the TD also called a Switcher? Is there a difference?
Yes. The term TD implies more than just operating the switcher—a TD takes a broader concern that all technical functions in the studio are operating properly. The DIR depends on the TD for technical support.

On the other hand, when a crew person is mainly operating the switcher and does not takes a broader concern for technical operation, then he or she is simply referred to as "switcher."

The switcher console has all the buttons and fader bars necessary to perform transitions between shots—cuts, fades, dissolves, wipes, and keys. Let's review those transitions:

A TD should understand what *black* is. A show begins in black and ends in black. However, black is not the absence of video. Rather, the color black is a video source that must be generated. Thus, when you wish to fade up from black or fade to black, you must select black as a source on your switcher.

The TD should understand basic transitions:

Cut - A cut is an immediate transition between shots—the shortest possible transition. A cut is performed by pushing the button of a different source on the same bank of buttons on the switcher. This provides an instant transition between sources, such as Camera 1 to Camera 2.

Dissolve - A dissolve is a cross-fade between scenes that involves more than one frame of transition time—in other words, anything longer than a cut. In a dissolve, you see part of one image fading away as another image comes into view. A dissolve rate can be measured in seconds or in frames. A thirty-frame dissolve is one second. Executing a dissolve involves moving the fader bar on the switcher from a selection on one row of buttons to a selection on the neighboring row of buttons.

Fade - Aesthetically, a fade refers to a dissolve up from black, such as you would see at the start of a show, or a dissolve to black, as you would expect to see at the end of a show. Executing a fade is the same as executing a dissolve, except that one of your two selections is always the button on the switcher that provides the color black. In summary, you *dissolve* between pictures; you *fade* to black or up from black.

Wipe - A wipe is a transition between shots that employs the use of a geometric pattern moving on the screen to reveal the new source. The pattern may be a box or circle that grows bigger, or it could be a line moving across the screen vertically or horizontally to reveal the next picture.

Like a dissolve, a wipe also involves more than one frame of transition time, moving the fader bar from one source to another, and seeing both shots on the scene at the same time, except in this case they are not superimposed on each other as in the dissolve. Instead, they are juxtaposed by way of the geometric pattern.

Computer-generated wipe patterns, called digital effects, lend a great deal of sophistication to the wipe transition. The traditional wipes were two-dimensional. The newer digital effects wipes have three dimensional attributes. Now, the geometric patterns appear to move in a 3-D environment: boxes flip and tumble, images shrink and expand or rotate on vertical axes like revolving doors. Images squeeze smaller while maintaining proportion.

Key - A key is an electronic cut-out of part of one image imposed over part of another. For example, if a person's name appears under his or her face while hosting a show, the letters of the name have been electronically inserted in the picture of the host. The letters come from the character generator; the face comes from the camera. The two images are combined in the key.

SETTING UP A KEY EFFECT ON THE SWITCHER

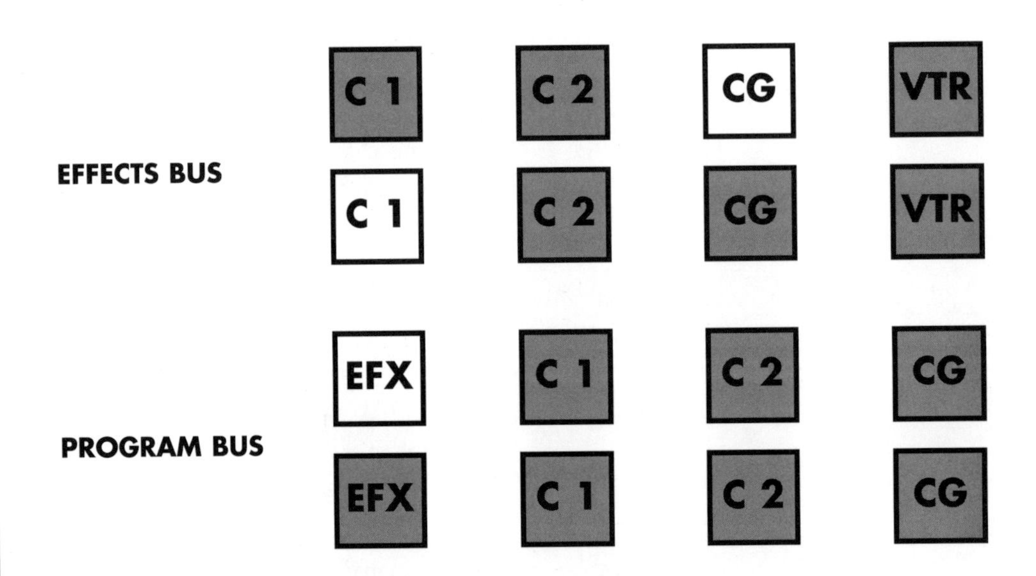

A switcher allows you to preset many kinds of effects including keys. To set up a key, "EFX" is selected on the main Program Bus. This enables any effect that is pre-set on the Effects Bus above. In this case, the pre-set effect is a key of Character Generator (CG) over Camera 1 (C1). Some switchers label their preset effects buttons as *mix/effects* or *ME*.

Wipes. A wipe is a geometric transition between two sources. On the left is a conventional 2-dimensional wipe. A box pattern slowly reveals the man's face. On the right is a digital wipe using a digital effects generator. In this case, the box image can be proportionally squeezed, rotated, flipped, and tumbled.

The Character Generator operator types a name ID to be keyed over the camera shot.

The name from the CG is keyed over the picture using the switcher.

The area in the lower part of the host's screen where a given letter appears must be electronically cut out and replaced with that letter. The electronic switcher does this. The operator sets up a key by designating which source appears over which other source.

The letters in the host's name are surrounded by black on the CG. The switcher ignores the black area and responds anywhere it sees the brighter video of the lettering. It cuts out the letters and cuts identically sized spaces out of the other picture. Then, like putting jigsaw puzzle pieces into place, the switcher inserts the images of the letters into corresponding holes in the other picture. The result is a composite picture—one source keyed over the other.

A key should be distinguished from a partial or half dissolve, which is simply a partial fade between two sources. In this case, you have 50% of one image superimposed over 50% of another image. With a key, however, 100% of part of one image is inserted into a source that maintains 100% of the rest of its image. In other words, the letters of the name are at 100% video level, inserted over the picture of the host which is also at 100% video level.

Character Generator Operator - CG

The *character generator* is a generic term for a computer that acts something like a word-processor to create words that appear on the screen. Newer CGs can also create graphic design elements as well. CGs are often referred to by brand name such as "Chyron" or "Dubner."

The CG operator should be proficient at typing and saving to disk any pages of names, credits, or other information needed for the show. If your studio does not have a CG, the crew member may be placed in charge of easel graphics, graphic slides, etc.

Announcer - ANNC

The *announcer* is available for live reading of announce copy. The announcer can be stationed either in the studio using a stand microphone, or in an announce booth.

Announcements can be pre-recorded and played back on tape. However the live announce offers you the spontaneous ability to shorten or lengthen the announcer time depending on how much time remains in the program. The live announcer may slow down, speed up, or cut sections of the copy at a moment's notice to accommodate time.

Floor Assistant - FA

The *floor assistant* or FA offers general assistance in the studio. It's always helpful to have an extra set of hands. The FA typically helps with:

- positioning easel graphics
- assisting camera moves by pulling and moving the large camera cables
- handling props

The Announcer may deliver a "live" announce or may prerecord an announcement.

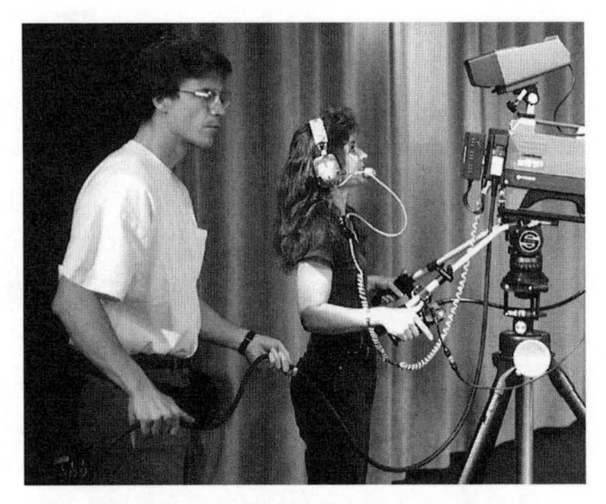

The Floor Assistant offers general help in the studio. Often, cables get tangled. The FA helps keep them clear.

Lighting Director - LD

The title of *lighting director* usually goes to the one who designs a lighting plot. Then, the *gaffers* and *grips* are the crew who actually climb the ladders and hang lighting instruments. In a smaller scale production, one person might do it all. In any case, the lighting director should be:

- familiar with basic lighting techniques
- familiar with lighting instruments and controls

If you're not familiar with basic *three-point lighting*—key light, fill light, back light—you may want to review this fundamental method for lighting a person's face. The rationale for three-point lighting to create some subtle but natural shadows on a person's face—the lighting is not too flat, yet not too shadowy. This type of lighting is much more pleasing and natural than a head-on harsh light which looks flat and washed out.

In three-point lighting, the *key light* is the primary light source. It is aimed at the subject from about forty-five degrees above and forty-five degrees to one side of the subject. The *fill light* is aimed at the subject's other side at about half the foot candles (intensity) of the key light. The theory is that a fill light at half intensity will help create natural shadows. The *back light* hits the subject from behind, also from about forty-five degrees above. The light should be aimed at the head and shoulders. The back light serves to highlight parts of the body that would otherwise fade into the background and appear flat. Highlighting the head and shoulders makes the person stand out from the background and gives the picture more depth.

There is no single way to light someone, but if you are aware of the principles of three-point lighting, then you have a basis from which to work and create your own variations.

A lighting grip places a key light on a floor stand.

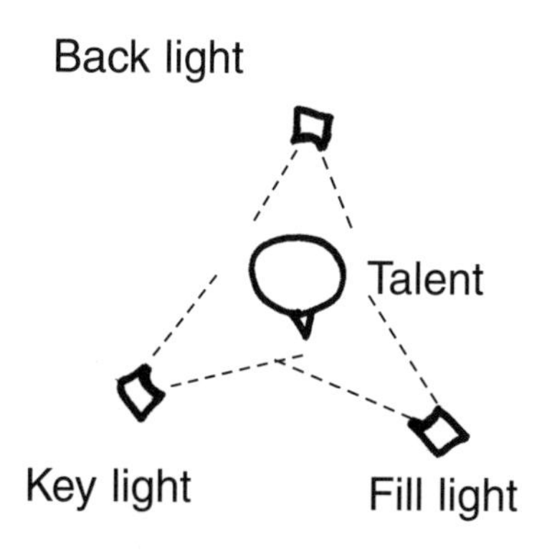

On-camera talent are usually lit using the three-point lighting technique. Lights may be hung from a ceiling grid or placed on floor stands.

Set Designer - SET

The set must first be constructed and then decorated. Typically, a construction crew of carpenters and electricians will build the set. Then, set decorators will take care of furnishings and props. The student production may not necessarily worry about set construction but may assign someone on the crew to make sure the set is clean and ready for the next crew rotation.

The Set Designer plans and constructs the set. Assistants and carpenters normally help with the actual construction.

Talent - TAL

The talent is anyone who is seen or heard in the production. You can refer to the person generically as "talent" or specifically by role: host, anchor, actor, etc.

Talent may be professional or non-professional. Sometimes the talent may have no TV experience and may need coaching from the director.

Talent is a generic term for any on-camera performer. In this case, the talent is a news anchor.

Cue cards/Prompter

Cue cards or electronic *teleprompters* allow the talent to read script copy while maintaining eye contact with the camera. If you have cue cards, the crew person should hold the cards next to the lens, scrolling as the talent reads..

Cue card material should be medium stiff white board cut into narrow vertical strips so that the talent's eyes don't have to wander sideways while reading.

If you have an electronic teleprompter, the operator should be quick at recuing to different points in the script.

Holding cue cards is a skill. The cards must be held and scrolled so that the talent's eyes stay near the lens.

Videotape Operator - VTR

The person in the VTR position is responsible for recording and playing back videotapes during the show. The director should call for a tape to start recording about 30 seconds to airtime so that the class has a record of the completed show as it would have been seen by viewers at home.

VTR playback segments may include: opening title sequences, closing title sequences, station ID bumpers going in and out of commercial breaks, news packages, and silent images for anchors to voice-over.

Videotape segments should be cued and ready to roll when the director gives the command. Normal practice is to cue the videotape segment anywhere from one to three seconds prior to the beginning of the segment. The roll cue is given by the director one to three seconds ahead of the actual transition to the videotape segment. That gives time for the playback VTR to come up to speed and for the image to stabilize.

The VTR operator is responsible for cuing up each segment the appropriate number of seconds ahead of the beginning, then leaving it cued and standing by for a roll cue. Upon hearing the director's roll cue, the VTR operator hits the play button. As soon as the tape rolls, the director waits for one to three seconds and then calls to the TD for a cut, dissolve, or wipe to the VTR.

SUMMARY

The crew is vital to the success of any program. Studio production affords you the chance to try out all these crew positions, to see which ones capture your interest. You might specialize in one area or generalize.

As a director, your experience with each crew position will help enormously in your directing ability. When crew members sense the director's understanding of their jobs, they tend to be more respectful and responsive.

This overview of crew responsibilities gives you an introduction to other jobs when you are not actually directing. Ideally, you will have the time early in the semester to try out each crew position and develop your skills.

PLANNING WORKSHEETS

Directing live television involves a lot of advance planning to conceptualize the flow of the show. The following chapters focus on skills and resources to help you with this advance planning.

For example, you need to decide who is on your crew, how the studio will be set, how the talent will be lit, how the microphones will be placed, how many segments in the show, the length of each segment, the types of camera shots for each segment, and the commands you will need to execute the live production. For these decisions, you can use various forms to help you plan.

In this chapter we'll start with some useful worksheets:

1. Crew List and Rotation Schedule
2. Floor Plan
3. Lighting Plot
4. Rundown
5. Segment timing sheet

You may make up your own versions of these worksheets or use generic blank forms that come with this book. Your professor may have a supply of blank forms as well.

CREW ROTATION SCHEDULE

As director, you need to know who is on your crew. You may be assigned a crew. Or you may choose your own crew. Either way, you need a crew roster to make sure everyone is accounted for and to let you know who to communicate with for any given crew position on your show.

At least, you should have a crew list for you own show. But since most classroom situations cycle through a series of directing exercises in a given day, it's helpful to know all the crew rotations for the day on one form.

The *crew list* or *crew rotation schedule* lets everyone know who is doing what job for any given show. With the rotation schedule, you can see what your crew position will be for each rotation throughout the day.

Ideally the rotation is structured so that you as director do not have to perform a crew function during the production preceding yours. That gives you time to sit out one rotation and do some last minute planning for your show. The "bye" position, indicated in the rotation schedule, allows the next director to do just that, to sit out for one round in order to prepare.

Each script exercise has its own specific crew requirements. One exercise may call for an announcer. Another may have pre-recorded announcements and no need for a live announcer. Some exercises have one talent. Others have two or three.

Part of your planning job as director is to figure out your crew needs. Try making your own generic list of all crew positions you can imagine. Then, for each show you direct, look over that list and see which positions you need for your show.

SAMPLE CREW ROTATION SCHEDULE

production date_____________ script/exercise _______________

AIR TIMES

CREW	1:00	1:15	1:30	1:45	2:00	2:15	2:30	2:45	3:00	3:15	3:30	3:45
BYE	Lee	Mo	Jan	Max	Tom	Dee	Joe	Don	Ann	Jim	Sue	Bob
DIR	Bob	Lee	Mo	Jan	Max	Tom	Dee	Joe	Don	Ann	Jim	Sue
AD	Sue	Bob	Lee	Mo	Jan	Max	Tom	Dee	Joe	Don	Ann	Jim
TD	Jim	Sue	Bob	Lee	Mo	Jan	Max	Tom	Dee	Joe	Don	Ann
AUD 1	Ann	Jim	Sue	Bob	Lee	Mo	Jan	Max	Tom	Dee	Joe	Don
CAM ①	Don	Ann	Jim	Sue	Bob	Lee	Mo	Jan	Max	Tom	Dee	Joe
CAM ②	Joe	Don	Ann	Jim	Sue	Bob	Lee	Mo	Jan	Max	Tom	Dee
FM	Dee	Joe	Don	Ann	Jim	Sue	Bob	Lee	Mo	Jan	Max	Tom
ANNC	Tom	Dee	Joe	Don	Ann	Jim	Sue	Bob	Lee	Mo	Jan	Max
TAL	Max	Tom	Dee	Joe	Don	Ann	Jim	Sue	Bob	Lee	Mo	Jan
CG	Jan	Max	Tom	Dee	Joe	Don	Ann	Jim	Sue	Bob	Lee	Mo
LD	Mo	Jan	Max	Tom	Dee	Joe	Don	Ann	Jim	Sue	Bob	Lee
VTR	Lee	Mo	Jan	Max	Tom	Dee	Joe	Don	Ann	Jim	Sue	Bob
SET	Bob	Lee	Mo	Jan	Max	Tom	Dee	Joe	Don	Ann	Jim	Sue

Notice that each name rotates one level down and to the right until everyone has been in every position.

FLOOR PLAN

Each script in this book is accompanied by a *floor plan*. You may use the particular plan out of the book, or create your own that better matches the dimensions of your studio.

The floor plan is a helpful tool for planning your production. With it you are able to:

1. Plan the studio set-up and design your set.
2. Visualize on paper what the set will look like and where the cameras will be positioned.

As you create your sequence of camera shots and moves, you can play out the scenarios on your floor plan using your imagination to determine whether your command sequence is realistic. Sketching it all out on a floor plan might clarify, for example, that C① is further away than C② from the easel graphic. Therefore the easel graphic shot will be assigned to C②.

You can make little paper cut-outs or models of cameras, furniture, and people to place on the floor plan and move them about as you visualize and plan your shots.

See if everything seems logical. Talk yourself through your script, imagining what is taking place on the set as each camera breaks for a new shot. You will be able to spot problems before they occur.

SAMPLE FLOOR PLAN

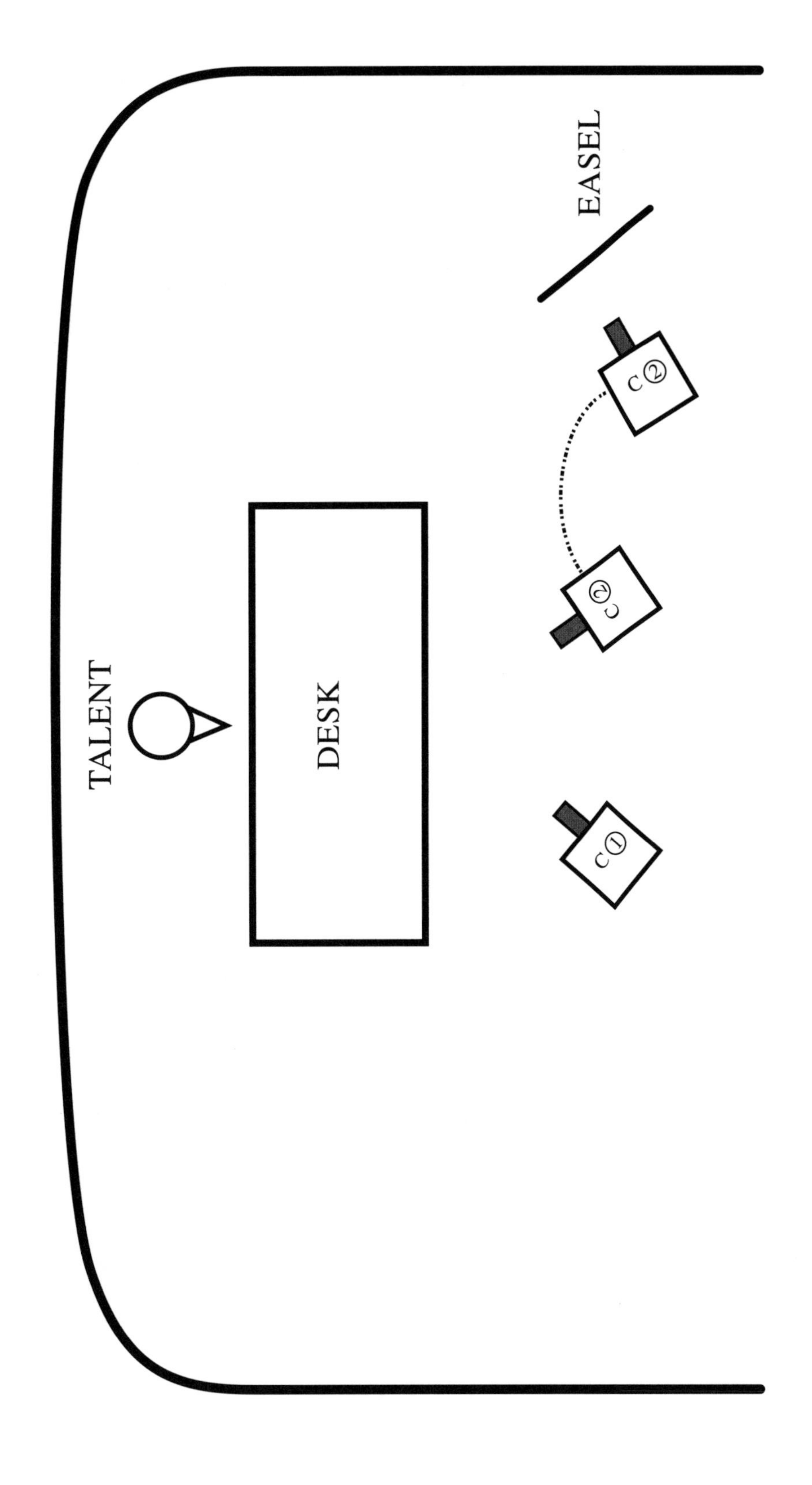

LIGHTING PLOT

If your class is rotating through the same exercise, the lighting may not need to change. However, once you advance from doing common exercises as a class to creating your own unique show, you will need to consider a lighting plot that is appropriate for your production. In other words, adjusting the lighting for your show becomes one of the necessary pre-production tasks. Therefore, it is good to know the importance of a lighting plot and to think about your lighting design.

A lighting director might do the actual design, but the TV director is ultimately responsible for the production and should be aware of the lighting design and approve it. In your class, you can use the form provided in this workbook or create your own lighting plot for each production. This form becomes a working map for hanging and aiming lighting instruments.

Start by sketching the basic furniture or position of the talent. Is there an easel stand for camera graphics? That needs to be lit as well. Draw in the location of key, fill, and back lights for each talent, and special lighting instruments for items such as the graphics stand.

From this plot, you know exactly what hardware is needed and where it should go. You may want to do an inventory of your studio's lighting instruments so you know what's available.

Lighting instruments generally fall into four categories:
• *focusable*, which means the light passes through a glass lens
• *non-focusable*, which means there is no lens and the light throw is much broader.
• *short-throw*, which means the instrument is designed to focus light in relatively short distances
• *long-throw*, which means the light will focus many yards away

So, for example, in a small studio, you may choose focusable short-throw instruments such as *fresnels* for key, fill, and back lights. You may chose to light your easel graphics with a non-focusable light such as a *scoop* for a general wash of light.

SAMPLE LIGHTING PLOT

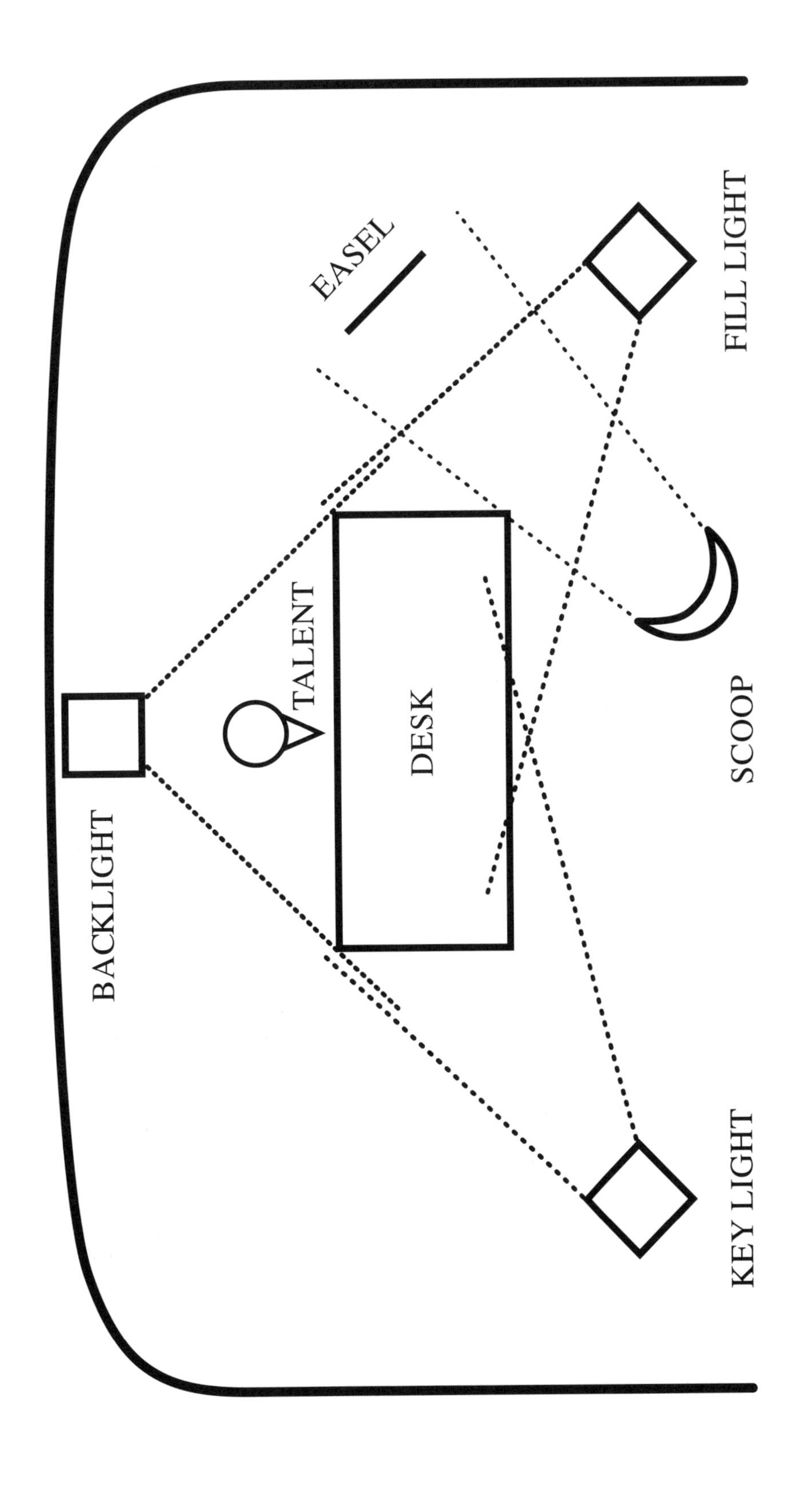

RUNDOWNS

TV News stations use both rundowns and scripts to direct the news. The script spells out the entire show word-for-word and the *rundown* summarizes all segments in an easy-to-read spread sheet.

The crew may not need to to know every word that is spoken by the news anchor. The crew would prefer to have a rundown, an abbreviated list of segments showing the technical needs for each segment. For example, the rundown quickly shows the VTR operator whether the following segment contains a VTR roll-in.

Whereas the crew may use rundowns and the anchors use scripts, the director uses both. The rundown is a good planning tool and a great way to stay on top of the order of segments as the show progresses. But while calling the shots, the script is the most important tool since it shows all spoken words.

Rundowns may come in the form of computer programs. The programs act like data bases and allow the director to fill in the cells with all the infor-

Rundown - 5:00 News

SEG	TALENT	STORY	VTR	Length
1	Bob	Tease	v/o mos	:30
2	Sue	Robbery	V/O SOT	1:00
3	Bob/Sue	Fire	V/OSOTV/O	:45
4	Reporter	Car chase	SOT	1:05
5	Bob	triplets	none	:25
6	Jim	Sports	V/O mos	1:30
7	Carol	Weather	none	2:00
8	Bob	Circus	V/O mos	:20
9	Bob/Sue	Tease	none	:15
C O M M E R C I A L B R E A K # 1				

mation needed. The sample rundown shows the segments up to and including the first commercial break of a live newscast:

SEGMENT TIMING SHEET

The *segment timing sheet* helps the director keep track of timing during each segment of the program. After each segment, the director should know whether the overall show is running on time or behind schedule. The segment timing sheet is useful tool for checking the time and making adjustments on upcoming segments throughout the show. Time cues are written in the grid to indicate time remaining for each segment: 3 minutes remaining, 2 minutes, 1 minute, wrap (15 seconds), and cut (5 seconds). Segment timing will be covered in detail in Chapter 6.

Segment	Length	IN	OUT	3	2	1	30	W	C

DIRECTING TALENT

AND CREW

The Director gives last-minute directions to the news anchor.

As director, you are the liaison between the technical side of the production and the conceptual side. It is not enough to just call shots and watch the monitor. The director must be satisfied with whatever is happening in the studio.

The director exercises much of the artistic control through direction given to the talent. Therefore, it's a good idea to greet your talent when they arrive, to rehearse with them, to give feedback on their performance, and to thank them after the show.

The talent depends on the director for a clear concept of the show. The director should take the initiative to explain his or her vision of how the show should go, as well as specific instructions: "Sit here, look to this camera," etc.

Be tactful. Don't announce over the PA system that the talent needs to do a better job. You may need to go out and speak quietly one-on-one in order to give constructive criticism.

Compliment your talent. Have your FM tell them that they look good, that they are doing a good job. The immediate emotional lift, timed properly, will carry over into the final product.

FMs should be fluent in hand signals which the talent can easily understand, such as: time remaining, slow down, speed up, change cameras.

The talent sometimes likes to respond to tally lights on cameras. They wait to talk until they see the red light. That is too unreliable. The TAL's camera tally may come on for some reason unknown to the TAL. The DIR may not

The director talks to CAM ① before the rehearsal gets underway. He explains his plan for framing and camera moves during the live newscast.

be cuing the TAL to begin yet. The DIR may be on a wide shot of the studio, for example, while the opening titles are finishing. Therefore, the TAL should be told to follow cues from the FM only, not from the tally lights.

Working with cameras

As director, you depend heavily on skilled execution by camera operators. You must give camera operators an idea of what to expect in your show. What needs to be practiced? What kind of framing do you want? During the show, the DIR may call for any number of actions including: zoom, pan, tilt, truck, dolly, break, and the camera ops should know how to respond.

At the same time, don't go overboard with detail. You won't have the time. Give them only as much as is necessary or as time allows.

Whenever a camera moves to a new scene, focus must be rechecked. The only way to get an accurate focus is to zoom all the way in to the subject, check focus, and then zoom back out to the desired field of view. Thus, the DIR should expect a quick focus check each time the camera breaks for a new scene and before the DIR calls for the take to the camera.

Camera operators should understand the difference between a "hot move" and a break for a new shot. When you say: "Camera ②, you're hot, pan to the other guest," that implies that the camera is on line and should execute the move as smoothly as possible. However, if you say,

"Camera ②, break for the other guest," that implies that Camera ② is off line and he or she should hurry to frame up the other guest.

It may seem overwhelming—all these people to deal with: TAL, TD, CAM, AUD, all needing to know what to do, yet you have such a limited amount of time. So, the biggest challenge is to do all this efficiently.

Make sure that you tell people what they need to hear, without wasting too much time. One tip for being efficient is to consider which items must be explained ahead of time and which items will become self-evident during rehearsal. For example, why waste time getting a precise audio level from the TAL? Why not just do a rehearsal and the audio person will fine tune the level during the rehearsal period?

Working with TD/switcher

As DIR, your TD is an extension of your arm, the one who pushes the buttons, fades up and down, keeps an eye on technical quality, and other things that you don't have the extra hands or eyes to do.

Try to establish a good system of communication. Go over any complex transitions. When you ask for a dissolve, do you mean fast, medium or slow? Give the TD the necessary information to preset any effects and to be aware of any other special concerns.

Working with audio

Your audio people will also need a few seconds of specific instructions. What audio sources are being used? Is there audio on VTR rolls? Do you want sneaks, fades, or hits on music cues? Is there any specific instruction about mic placement in the studio?

Audio is a major component of your show. It's easy to overlook audio and focus on the visual component of the show, but any good TV show has good audio as well.

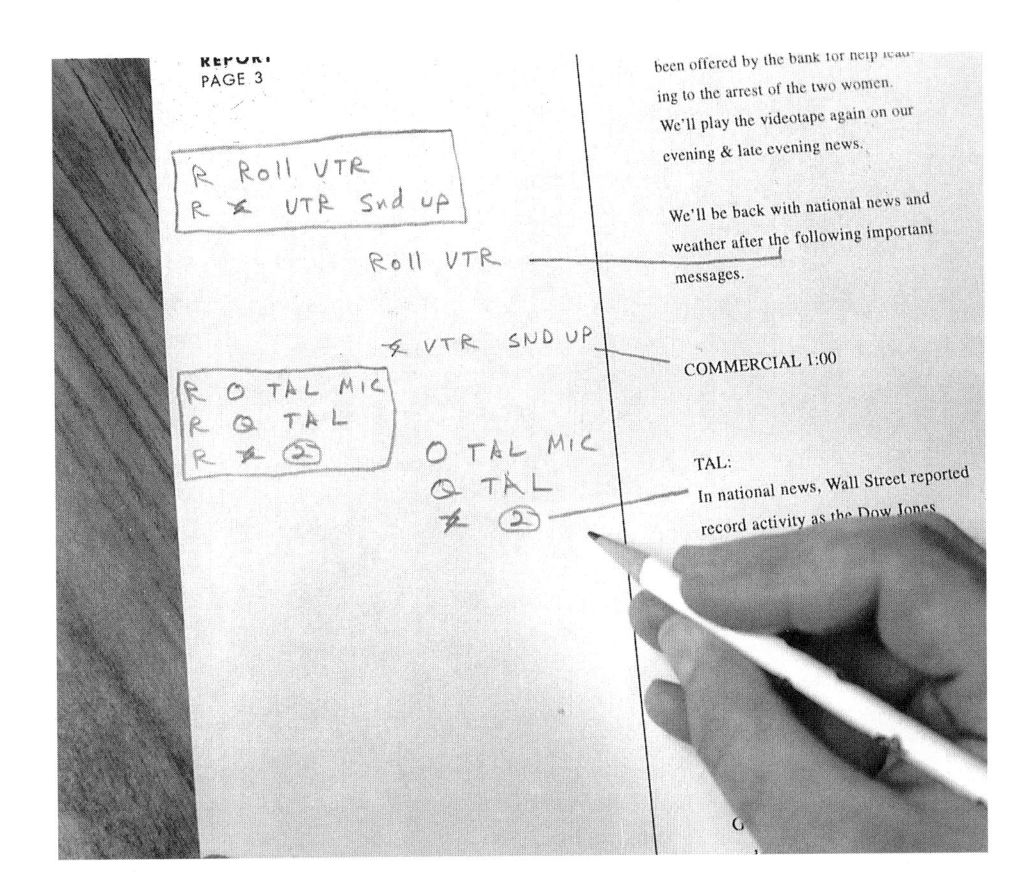

SCRIPTS AND

SCRIPT-MARKING

Just as a symphony conductor may refer to a music score with notations while conducting, the TV director refers to a script with all appropriate commands penciled in the margin.

The goal in this section is to teach a basic script-marking protocol that serves two purposes:

1. It gives you a useful shorthand so that your scripts are not covered with long-hand scribbles which are difficult to read and refer to quickly.
2. It teaches you a standard language that is understood throughout the industry.

The TV industry does not always use protocol as detailed and specific as you will learn here. People form their own unique habits over time, especially within familiar work environments. For example, within a given TV station, the staff who is used to working together may have formulated their own variations of commands. Often, the routine is so familiar, day after day, that many commands become unspoken.

There is, however, a set of universally recognized commands. These become especially important when you find yourself in a new situation and you cannot assume that the crew knows what to do.

Whereas the rundown is useful for planning, the script is where all the director's commands are actually written. Some productions will be fully scripted; some will be partially scripted, leaving room for free-form elements such as interviews or unscripted demonstrations.

Not all professional situations will use the same script format. Some use separate audio and video columns. Some use one column on one side of the page. In this book, the scripts have everything in one column, leaving the other column blank for you to write your notations. This is a typical live studio production format.

Notice that every script is at least double spaced. You will want ample room to write your command notation. Also notice that each script begins about halfway down the first page. In almost every script, you will have preparation notes. This half page of extra room on page 1 will give you room for those notes.

Now, let's learn the shorthand that will allow you to mark your scripts with all the commands you will need to direct your show from beginning to end including: shot transition, music cues, and talent cues.

Script-marking is based on the notion that a director first *"readies"* a command and then actually executes it. As often as possible, you should "ready" every command. In other words, every command gets delivered twice, first as a ready, then as the actual command.

For example, "Ready ②" means you will soon take to Camera ②. Then, when the moment comes, the DIR says, "Take ②," and the switcher, who knew the command was on its way, has his or her finger on the right button ready to go. It is wise to ready all your commands, no matter how minuscule they may seem. Then, as your work environment becomes more familiar, you can trim or simplify the number of commands needed as your crew knows better what to expect. For example, any one-time-only TV special will have commands unfamiliar to the crew. But a regular series, such as a sit-com, may have sets of commonly repeated commands that may not always need to be readied. Use your judgment.

You will notice different protocols at different TV stations. Some will say "stand by" instead of ready. Some will rarely say a ready. But that is only typical of a production in which the crew is intimately familiar with the process and does the news as a team night after night. However, many situations are not so familiar and you're best bet is to ready most commands.

The following are some commonly used shorthand terms for director's commands. You may modify these terms. The point is to write these commands on your script as cleanly and concisely as possible. A cluttered script is hard to read. The shorthand makes commands not only easy to write, but quick and easy to speak.

SCRIPT-MARKING SHORTHAND

Commands

Ready	= R	Take	= T
Cue	= Q	Dissolve	= X
Open	= O	Microphone	= MIC
Roll	= ROLL	Fade	= F
Music	= MUS	Effects	= EFX
Lavaliere	= LAV	Announcer	= ANNC
Talent	= TAL	Camera	= ①, ②, etc.
VTR	= VTR	Film	= FILM
Tape	= TAPE	Picture(s)	= PIX, PIC
Zoom	= ZM	Background	= BKGND

Fade Sound & Picture Out = FSAPO

Music can hit (HIT), sneak (SNK), fade (F), to background (BKGND)

Camera framing terms

Close-up	= CU
Cover shot	= CS
Extreme close-up	= ECU
Over the shoulder	= OS
Head and shoulders	= HS
Medium shot	= MS
Waist shot	= WS
Knee shot	= KS
Full Figure	= FF

Camera moves

Pan	(Pan Left or Right)
Tilt	(Tilt Up or Down)
Zoom	(Zm In or Out)
Dolly	(Dolly In or Out)
Truck	(Trk Left or Right)
Arc	(Arc Left or Right)

Next, let's see how these commands look when written on a script.

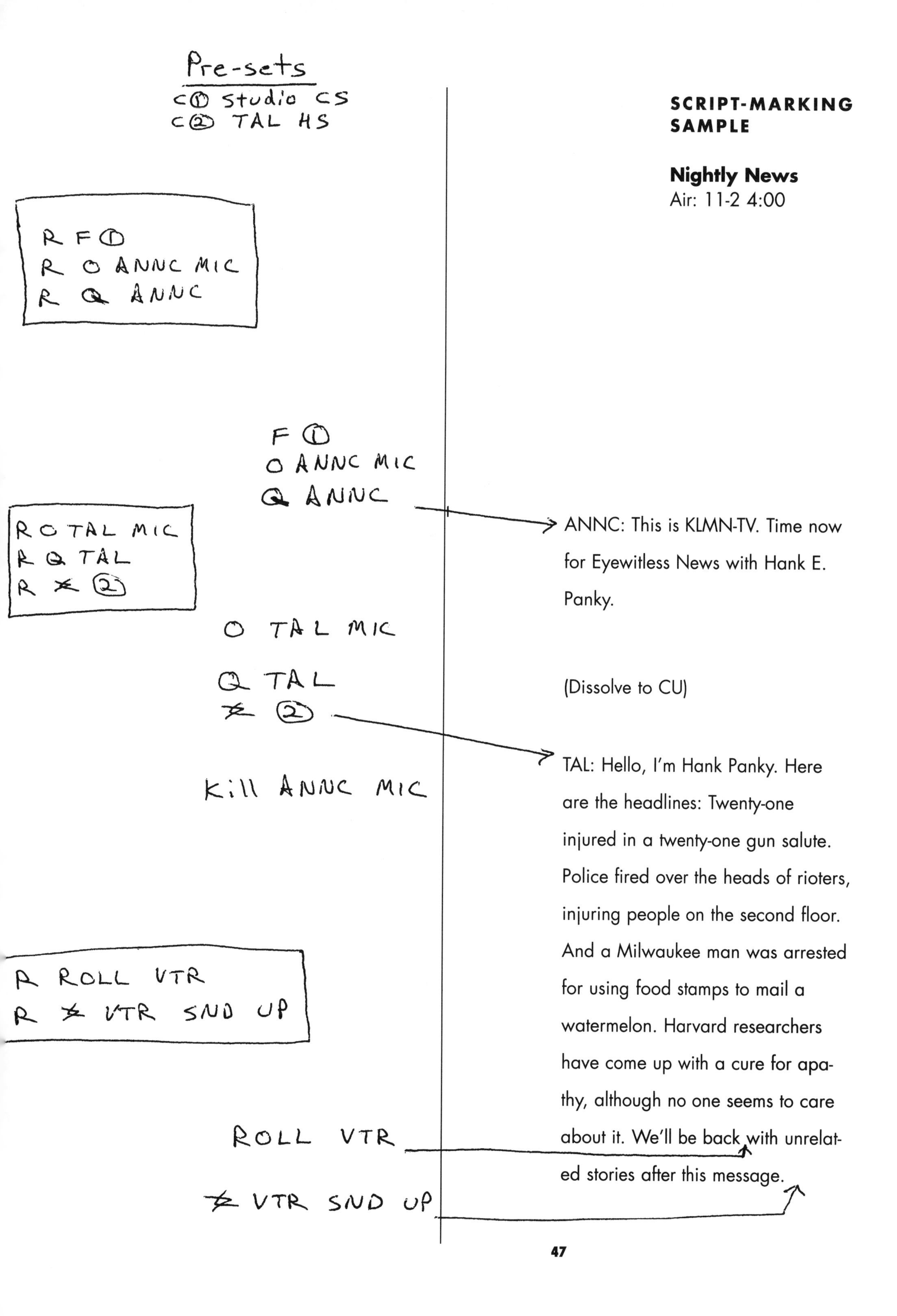
Pre-sets
C① Studio CS
C② TAL HS
R F①
R O ANNC MIC
R Q ANNC
F①
O ANNC MIC
Q ANNC
R O TAL MIC
R Q TAL
R ✕ ②
O TAL MIC
Q TAL
✕ ②
Kill ANNC MIC
R ROLL VTR
R ✕ VTR SND UP
ROLL VTR
✕ VTR SND UP
SCRIPT-MARKING SAMPLE
Nightly News
Air: 11-2 4:00
ANNC: This is KLMN-TV. Time now for Eyewitless News with Hank E. Panky.
(Dissolve to CU)
TAL: Hello, I'm Hank Panky. Here are the headlines: Twenty-one injured in a twenty-one gun salute. Police fired over the heads of rioters, injuring people on the second floor. And a Milwaukee man was arrested for using food stamps to mail a watermelon. Harvard researchers have come up with a cure for apathy, although no one seems to care about it. We'll be back with unrelated stories after this message.

EXPLANATION OF SHORTHAND

On the previous page, you saw examples of commands written on page 1 of a script. Now, here is a full list of commonly used commands and shorthand.

R - READY

The purpose of ready commands is to let crew members anticipate and prepare for their next responses.

Most commands are preceded by "ready" commands. You say, "Ready Dissolve ①" before the actual command, "Dissolve ①." Or you can say groups of ready commands, "Ready Cue Talent, ready Dissolve ①," followed soon after by the actual commands: "Cue Talent, Dissolve ①."

Readies are essential to warn crew of imminent commands. The only danger is in confusing "ready" commands with actual commands, so make your speech clear.

Write all ready commands to the left and draw a box around groups of ready commands. This is an easy way to set them apart from actual commands.

Certain spontaneous commands to your crew such as "Camera ①, pan right" need not always be readied first. Use your judgment, but as a rule, ready as much as is reasonably possible.

T - TAKE

A take is a cut, as opposed to a dissolve or wipe. You can T①, T②, T VTR, etc. Take ① means cut to camera ①. That is a command for the TD to select C① on the switcher. Don't say, "Take Camera ①." That's three extra syllables at a time when you want to be as succinct as possible. Example as you would write in your script:

R①

T①

Spoken as: "Ready 1, Take 1"

Q - CUE

Generally, you will say "Q" for cuing people: announcers, talent, anchors, hosts, etc. Cuing a tape machine is a little different. When you "Cue" a VTR or audio tape, that usually implies finding the right spot on the tape to begin. For an actual command to begin action, you "Roll" tape machines and "Q" talent.

Example:

R Q TAL

Q TAL

Spoken as: "Ready cue talent. Cue talent."

⋊ - DISSOLVE

Dissolve means that the TD will move the fader bar from one bank to the next on the switcher when executing a gradual shot transition, thus creating a dissolve. Dissolves can be slow or fast. Let your TD know what you have in mind.

Example:

R ⋊ ①

⋊ ①

Spoken as: "Ready dissolve 1. Dissolve 1."

O - OPEN

You "Open" microphones. It's a command to the AUDIO person to switch on a microphone channel on the mixer.

Example:

R O MIC

O MIC

Spoken as: "Ready open mic. Open mic"

Make sure you don't leave a mic open indefinitely. When the TAL is finished, give a command to CLOSE, CUT, or KILL the mic.

F - FADE

Fade is a command to the TD to go to black or up from black. As stated earlier, note the difference between fades and dissolves. They both involve moving the fader bar on the switcher from one bank to the other. However, it's helpful to distinguish between a dissolve, which goes from image to image, and a fade which goes from image to black, or from black to image. This distinction of "fade" helps immediately identify that you're beginning or ending a segment or a program.

Example:

R F②

F ②

Spoken as: "Ready fade in 2. Fade in 2."

ROLL

A cue to start tape machines—VTRs or audio tape machines. "ROLL VTR" or "ROLL MUS TAPE"

Example:

R ROLL VTR

ROLL VTR

MUS - MUSIC

Music can be on record, cassette, CD, videotape, reel-to-reel tape, or live.

HIT MUS - HIT MUSIC

Hit Music means the fader is already up on the audio board so that when you roll a tape machine or cue a record, the music will come in at full level instead of fading in.

Example:

R HIT MUS

HIT MUS

MIC - MICROPHONE

Microphones can be announce booth mics, table top mics, lavalieres or lapel mics, shotgun mics or hand held mics.

LAV - LAVALIERE

You could specify "O LAV" instead of "O MIC" if one is being used. Be clear which mics you want open if there are several. You can also identify a mic by the TAL who is using it.

Example:

R O ANNC MIC

O ANNC MIC

ANNC - ANNOUNCER

The announcer may be in an announce booth, or out in the studio standing at a mic. The announcer gets his or her cue relayed by the floor manager if on the floor, or by the director through headphones if in an announce booth.

Example:

R Q ANNC

Q ANNC

EFX - EFFECTS

An effect is a combination of video sources within one picture such as a wipe, a key, or a superimposition. For example, an effect could be a key of words from the CG over CAM ① to identify someone speaking. The key is created at the switcher.

An effect should be preset. You can select your combination of sources, assign them to a certain location on the switcher, and then have that effect all ready to dissolve or cut to.

Imagine that a TAL is about to get his or her name keyed. The director must find time in the production to make sure the effect is preset. Then when the time comes, the director need not waste precious time saying "Dissolve effects of CG over 1," but simply "Dissolve Effects," written in shorthand notation: "⨯ EFX."

Example:

R ⨯ EFX

⨯ EFX

TAL - TALENT

Talent is any person being seen or heard in the program. You may specify which TAL by calling them ANNC, HOST, ANCHOR, GUEST, etc.

①, ② - CAM ①, CAM ②.

A circled number always means a camera. You can save room on your script by not writing out the word "camera."

Example:

R ⨯ ②

⨯ ②

VTR - VIDEO TAPE RECORDER OR PLAYBACK

VTRs can be used to playback roll-in news packages or commercials. TV studios often use more than one VTR playback machine, so they will number or letter them, such as: "ROLL VTR-A, or ROLL VTR-B."

For both VTR and film, you roll the machine about three seconds before taking or dissolving to it. Therefore, you have two sets of commands.

Example:

R Roll VTR R ⨯ VTR

ROLL VTR (Say by the time the countdown reaches "3.")
⨯ VTR (Say by the time the countdown reaches "1.")

FILM - FILM CHAIN

Your studio may have a film chain or telecine in addition to VTR playback. You can roll a film the same way you would roll a VTR for playback.

TAPE

This usually refers to audio tape. Say "ROLL TAPE" if you mean audio tape, "ROLL VTR" if you mean videotape. You may wish to use another distinguisher for audio tape, such as "ATR" for audio tape recorder.

PIC OR PIX - PICTURE(S)

This usually refers to an easel card—a graphic or picture out in the studio on an easel for the camera to frame. Pictures can be changed by the FM or FA while the camera is momentarily off line.

Example:

R Change PIC

Change PIC

ZM - ZOOM

Mark the places in your script where you want zooms to occur.

BKGND - BACKGROUND

A cue for MUS. You might start with music up full, then bring it to background before ANNC.

MUS BKGND - MUSIC TO BACKGROUND

This means bring the sound level down to a point where the voice of an announcer or talent will be clearly heard above it. Then wait for a command to fade out, sneak out, or swell.

Example:

R MUS BKGND

MUS BKGND

F MUS (IN OR OUT) - FADE MUSIC

This means moving the fader on the audio mixer up or down to bring the music level up or down.

Example:

R F MUS IN

F MUS IN

SNK MUS (IN OR OUT) - SNEAK MUSIC

This refers to a slow and subtle fade. The director may give some direction for how prolonged the sneak should be.

Example:

R SNK MUS OUT

SNK MUS OUT

SWELL MUS - SWELL MUSIC

Swell the music back up to a full level from a background level.

FSAPO - FADE SOUND AND PICTURE OUT

Don't say "Fah-sah-poh." That sounds funny. Instead, say the full command "Fade sound and picture out." This is the final curtain. In one quick command you have told the TD to fade to black, and the AUD to fade out all sound. Your show is now over.

Example:

R FSAPO

FSAPO

Commands rarely come one at a time. They usually come in groups. Therefore, you should write readies and commands in groups where appropriate.

On the following page, you'll see some examples of sets of commands that would typically go together. Notice the shorthand. But also notice why certain groups are grouped in certain orders. Ready commands are always in a box and located to the left of the actual commands.

Also, see appendices for examples of fully marked scripts.

SAMPLE COMMAND GROUPINGS

Ready open talent mic =
Ready Music =
Ready Cue Talent =
Ready Fade in ① =

R O TAL MIC
R MUS
R Q TAL
R F ①

O TAL MIC
Hit MUS
Q TAL
F ①
MUS OUT

Ready ② =

R ②

T ②

Ready dissolve ① =

R ✕ ①

✕ ①

Ready roll VTR track up =
Ready dissolve VTR track up =
Ready kill talent mic =

R ROLL VTR TRACK UP
✕ VTR TRACK UP
R KILL TAL MIC

ROLL VTR
✕ VTR TRACK UP
KILL TAL MIC

Ready open talent mic =
Ready cue talent =
Ready dissolve ② =
Ready music out =

R O TAL MIC
R Q TAL
R ✕ ②
R MUS OUT

O TAL MIC
Q TAL
✕ ②
MUS OUT

Ready Cue Announcer =
Ready ✕ ③ =
Ready music =
Ready kill talent mic =

R Q Annc
R ✕ ③
R MUS
R KILL TAL MIC

HIT MUS
Q ANNC
✕ ③
KILL TAL MIC

Ready fade sound
& picture out =

R FSAPO

FSAPO

How would you mark this script?

SCRIPT-MARKING PRACTICE

Nightly News
Page 1

ANNC: This is KLMN-TV. Time now for Eyewitless News with Hank E. Panky

(Dissolve to CU)

TAL: Hello, I'm Hank Panky. Here are the headlines: Twenty-one injured in a twenty-one gun salute. Police fired over the heads of rioters, injuring people on the second floor. And a Milwaukee man was arrested for using food stamps to mail a watermelon. Harvard researchers have come up with a cure for apathy, although no one seems to care about it. We'll be back with unrelated stories after this message.

(COMMERCIAL VTR-A 60 sec.)

TAL: During a white house press conference today, the president denied denying any denials. When asked which denial he was denying, the president denied comment.

(TED KOPPEL PIC)

And official word in from ABC news headquarters in New York—Ted Koppel has decided to comb his hair the other way. This change of part will first be seen on this Friday's Nightline. Koppel is believed to have switched barbers sometime in the last few days. And now for the weather. Tonight, a chance of partly and a bit of mostly. That's our news for tonight. Join me again tomorrow night for another Eyewitless News.

(MUSIC / COVER SHOT)

ANNC: This has been Eyewitless News with Hank E. Panky. You're watching KLMN-TV, where news is us.

SEGMENT TIMING

The AD keeps track of segment timing for the director.

Most shows, especially broadcast shows, have prescribed time lengths. A show that is scheduled to run 27:30 cannot run 27:40. So how do you stay on time?

This section explains methods for monitor time throughout your show in order to end exactly at the right moment.

Timing your show is not suggested for the first three exercises in Part II—so ADs, relax, you don't have to master timing right away. It is a skill that should be introduced after students are comfortable with more fundamental directing skills. So whether you use the following information now or later, at least you can begin to see what segment timing is all about.

The tool for achieving precise timing is the *segment timing sheet*. The director plans the segments and makes up the worksheet. The AD administers it in production, counting down segments, keeping the director apprised of segments ending early or late, and ultimately counting down the final ten seconds of the show.

Segment timing requires a method known as *back timing*—determining the amount of time remaining in any given segment of the show. It is less important to know how far into a segment you are; it is more important to know how much time you have left.

SAMPLE SEGMENT TIMING SHEET

Segment	Length	IN	OUT	3	2	1	30	W	C
OPEN									
NEWS									
COMM									
WTHER									
CLOSE									

Many people get quite confused with back timing at first. It is easy to get lost in the numbers, so practice ahead of time before the actual in-class exercise. Imagine that a segment is ending early or late. Are you able to use the segment timing sheet and the clock to figure out where you are? Can you advise the director properly, "We got out of that segment ten seconds late!"

The idea behind segment timing is to count down individual segments throughout the show so that the last segment will ultimately end the show right on time. In other words, if the director has no idea whether the show is on time or not until the last ten seconds, there is no time to collect thoughts and make changes.

However, if the director knows early in the show that timing is off, then he or she has more time and several segments over which to make up the time. For example, if segment 2 runs short, then the director can mention to the talent during the commercial to stretch a little in segment four. Or, the director can simply anticipate a longer stretch of music at the end and possibly delay the announcer cue by a few seconds.

The segment timing sheet does not have a standard format in the industry. You will see variations. In some cases, people may use a separate sheet like the one provided here. In other cases, the information from the sheet may be incorporated into the rundown or may be automated on computer.

First, let's look at each element of the segment timing sheet, then see how it all comes together on the form.

You might wish to study the sample form, then refer to the definitions that follow:

SEGMENT - Fill in this box with the name of the segment, such as: "open," "commercial," or "news."

LENGTH - What is the overall assigned length for that segment? For example, the open is :15, the commercial is :30, etc.

IN - What time does the segment begin within the running time of the show? For example, the commercial begins one minute after the start of the show, so the IN is "1:00."

OUT - What time within the running time of the show does the segment end? For example, a :30 commercial may end at 1:30 into the show.

3 - Three minutes to the end of the segment.

2 - Two minutes to end of segment.

1 - One minute to end of segment.

30 - Thirty seconds to end of segment.

W - Wrap segment - fifteen seconds to end of segment.

C - Cut - five seconds to end of segment.

Why Wrap and Cut? Why not just say "15 sec" and "5 sec"?
Either is fine. Traditionally, a host is given a WRAP sign as either a fist in the air or a circular motion above the head by the FM to indicate fifteen seconds left. That is the talent's cue to break from the interview and make closing remarks. The "Cut" sign, signaled by a slash of the throat, tells the talent that he or she has just enough time to say one or two more sentences. The TAL should finish within the following five seconds. Five seconds leaves enough time to say a couple of sentences such as, "Thank you for joining us. See you next week."

Segments differ from each other. Some need time cues given to TAL. Some do not. In the case of a free form interview, a host is looking for back timing signals from the floor manager so that he or she can pace the interview to end on time. However, in the case of a scripted segment, the talent does not need to be apprised of countdown times. In these cases, it is mainly the concern of the AD to communicate to the director how much time remains. If the segment is running long, the talent may get a cue to cut a certain section from the script to save time.

ADs—think about whom you are addressing for time cues. In the case of an interview segment, your job is to tell the FM over the headsets to "show 3 minutes" to the host, when there are three minutes remaining in the segment then "show two minutes," "show one minute," "show thirty" "show wrap," and "show cut."

However, in the case of a scripted segment, the floor manager is not going to have an impact on time. Instead, time is in the director's control only. In these cases, the AD addresses the director using language such as: "Thirty seconds to end of commercial," "fifteen to end of weather segment," and "5,4,3,2,1" to indicate to the time the segment should be over. If the show is running behind, the AD may follow with a remark such as, "We got out of the weather segment fifteen seconds late."

Be tactful in how you communicate in the control room. Don't upstage your director. Instead, edge in your cues around the director's commands. Be assertive and clear, but try not to step on toes.

How many segments should a show have?
There is no rule about how many segments a show should have. One director might choose to break a show down into nine segments. Another director might break the same show into four segments. It's up to you—whatever helps you direct your show and get out on time.

What is the difference between using a stopwatch or the clock on the wall? Either is OK—one gives you time from zero; the other gives you the time of day.

Time from zero means that the show starts at 00:00—the beginning of a stopwatch, even though the clock on the wall says 4:15 P.M. This method is handy when you know you have a reliable stopwatch system available in the control room. With this system, every segment timing sheet will begin its first segment at 00:00. A three-minute show will end at 3:00 on the stopwatch as well as on the segment timing sheet.

Or, you can fill in your segment timing sheet using the time of day. The same three-minute show, for example, begins at 4:15 P.M. and ends at 4:18 P.M. Segments are broken down on your form in relation to those times. Let's look at examples of each.

EXAMPLES OF SEGMENT TIMING

VERSION #1 using stopwatch time (Program begins at ZERO)

Segment	Length	IN	OUT	3	2	1	30	W	C
OPEN	:15	00:00	00:15						00:10
NEWS	1:00	00:15	1:15				:45	1:00	1:10
COMM	:30	1:15	1:45					1:30	1:40
WEATHER	1:00	1:45	2:45				2:15	2:30	2:40
CLOSE	:15	2:45	3:00						2:55

VERSION #2 using clock time (Program begins at time of day)

Segment	Length	IN	OUT	3	2	1	30	W	C
OPEN	:15	4:15:00	4:15:15						4:15:10
NEWS	1:00	4:15:15	4:16:15				4:15:45	4:16:00	4:16:10
COMM	:30	4:16:15	4:16:45					4:16:30	4:16:40
WEATHER	1:00	4:16:45	4:17:45				4:17:15	4:17:30	4:17:40
CLOSE	:15	4:17:45	4:18:00						4:17:55

NOTES ON THE SEGMENT TIMING SHEET EXAMPLES

Each line of the segment timing sheet refers only to that segment. As you follow across a line, you are looking at 30 seconds remaining, 15 seconds remaining, 5 seconds remaining of *that segment only*. Once that segment is over, you begin back-timing the next segment.

If the host is conducting a thirty minute interview, he or she may want a time check about halfway through the interview, but it doesn't have to be absolutely precise. A five-minute cue does not have to be exactly on the five-minute mark. Plus or minus a few seconds will not throw anyone off. But, as you get closer to the end, the time signals should be more accurate.

At the same time, floor managers should not distract the talent by wildly waving time cues. The holding up of fingers or time cards should be:

1. subtle but clear. Don't distract the talent with your movement.
2. in line with the talent's natural line of sight. In other words, floor managers should position themselves in a place where talent will hardly have to move an eyeball in order to catch the time cue.
3. in the case of an interview, time cues can be shown when the host is not speaking. The camera is likely to be on the guest, and, during the answer to a question, any eye movement by the host noticing the cue would be off camera.

Remember, time cues are usually shown to talent for unscripted segments such as interviews and demonstrations. A scripted segment's length is determined by the script. Instead of showing time cues, you make alterations in the script during rehearsal. Alterations in scripted segment time are made by:

1. Asking the talent to read faster or slower.
2. Cutting or adding copy to the script.

Normally, showing cues to a talent during a scripted segment does not accomplish much. In the case of these scripted segments, the timing sheet is mainly a tool for the director and AD in the control room to use among themselves.

Notice that you don't always fill in all the "time remaining" boxes on the segment timing sheet. It doesn't make much sense to give cues at 2:00 for a segment that's only 1:00 in length. Use your own judgment. Do whatever helps you and seems to make sense. For example, a 10-minute interview may need signals starting at 3:00 remaining. On the other hand, a

1-minute segment may require cues starting at 30 seconds remaining.
For a 1:00 commercial, the goal is simply to get out of it on time. As AD, you can warn the director at :30 remaining, then again at :20 or :15 remaining, then count down the final 10 seconds to the DIR.

CROSS CHECK YOUR WORK ON THE SEGMENT TIMING SHEET

1. Looking at the IN/OUT columns, the IN time of a new segment is always the OUT time of the previous segment.

2. The first IN time represents the beginning of the show; the last OUT time represents the end of the show. In the case of a clock time representation, this first IN and last OUT reflect the actual time on the clock at which you begin and end your show.

3. The CUT is always five seconds prior to the OUT time of the segment. The WRAP time is always fifteen seconds prior to the OUT time of that segment. The thirty second cue is always thirty seconds prior to the end of that segment. Check the example above to see these principles in action.

The following segment timing sheet has five mistakes. Can you find them?

Segment	Length	IN	OUT	3	2	1	30	W	C
OPEN	:15	3:00:00	3:00:15					3:00:05	3:00:10
NEWS	1:00	3:00:15	3:02:15				3:00:45	4:01:00	3:01:10
COMM	:30	3:01:15	3:01:45					3:01:30	4:01:40
WEATHER	1:00	3:01:45	3:02:45				3:02:15	3:02:30	3:02:40
CLOSE	:15	3:02:45	3:03:00						3:03:50

COMPOSITION

AND ESTHETICS

It's not enough for the director to say, "Give me a shot of the talent." The director must be more specific. Is it a close-up? A wide shot? From what angle?

Camera shots are categorized by:
• how wide the field of view is relative to the subject (wide angle versus telephoto)
• the camera's angle to the subject (low angle, eye level, or high angle)

With these two parameters alone, you, as director, can be extremely specific about the shot you want:
"Camera 2, give me a medium shot of the talent at eye level."

Imagine a studio production in which an artist is demonstrating some picture mounting techniques at a table-top. What are some possible shot types:

Cover Shot (CS) - A *cover shot,* also called an *establishing shot,* is a wide shot used for introducing the scene so that the viewer can see the entire context. It can be frustrating for the viewer to be introduced to a close-up and never have a chance to see the bigger environment. So, in this example, a cover shot would include the artist and the table, also showing enough of the room to see where he is, without making the shot so wide that the artist appears dwarfed. You may only need this establishing shot once at the beginning for a few seconds. Or, perhaps you might come back to it after a commercial in order to refresh the viewer's memory of the surroundings.

Medium Shot (MS) - The *medium shot* uses a longer focal length lens or a closer zoom position. Now, we see still see the artist and the table-top. However, the framing is significantly tighter than the cover shot. We don't see much of the room anymore. The artist, or talent, appears much larger in the frame. This is pleasing to the viewer. TV is a close-up medium and begs to move in closer. Although the viewer needs to see the cover shot, he or she doesn't want to linger on it, but wants to move on to the medium shot. As director, you can move from one to the other either by having your camera zoom in slowly, or by cutting to another camera already framed tighter on the medium shot.

Close-up (CU) - The *close-up* uses an even greater focal length or closer zoom. Now the artist's head and shoulders fills the frame.

Extreme Close-up (ECU) - A close-up may not be close enough. The closest possible framing is called the *extreme close-up*. In this shot, the artist's face fills the frame and even cuts off the top of the head.

Extreme close-ups are very intimate. An ECU may not be appropriate for a news or educational program. It may, however, by suitable for a dramatic scene.

It's best not to cut to ECUs from wide shots. Work your way in close and out wide through a sequences of shots.

There is no absolute rule of measurement to say where a cover shot ends and a medium shot begins. These are approximations. As director, you and your camera operator can decide what constitutes wide and medium, close, and extreme close.

Angles can be low, straight on, or high. As director, you must specify what angle you desire. Your choice of angle may be purely creative or purely practical. On the creative side, you may choose a high angle because it is visually interesting, stimulating, or unique. On the practical side, you must consider which angle best shows your subject matter. If a piece of machinery is best understood by looking at its operation from above, then your best choice as director is to frame a high angle.

FRAMING A PERSON

People are such common subjects in any television production, learning to frame a person or people is essential. First, think about your field of view. How much of the subject will you see in your framing? If you want to see the entire body, use a *full-figure* or *FF* shot. A shot cropped at the waist is a *waist shot* or *WS*. A nice framing for a portrait is a *head and shoulders shot* or *H/S*. A *close-up, CU,* eliminates most of the shoulders, and an *extreme close-up, ECU,* makes the face fill the screen.

Full Figure (FF)

Waist Shot (WS)

Head & Shoulders (H/S)

Close-up (CU)

Extreme Close-up (ECU)

It isn't enough to pick a field of view. You still have to fine tune the location of the head within the frame. You could place the head further up the screen, further down, further left, or further right. The head could be angled in any number of directions. How do you decide? Here are a few rules of thumb:

THE ONE THIRD RULE FOR EYES

On a medium, close, or extreme close-up, the subject's eyes should appear at about one third of the way down the screen. On a full-figure, the eyes may be higher than one-third.

HEAD ROOM

On any shot that shows the top of the head, the head should not touch the top of the frame. Instead, have the camera operator give a little bit of extra margin to create a separation between the top of the head and the top of the frame. This margin is called *head room*. The only time head room is not required is on an ECU in which the camera zooms in past the top of the head and intentionally cuts it off.

Here's another way to think about framing an ECU: The area from the eyes down to the mouth and chin—the lower half of the face—are the most visually important parts of the face. The eyes and mouth do all the communicating. So they should always have a prominent spot in the frame. Better to cut off the top of the head than to cut off part of the chin.

LOOK SPACE

Look space is extra room on the side of the frame which the subject is facing. If the subject is facing the camera, look space is not an issue. Some directors like to exaggerate look space and frame the shot with large amounts of excess room by placing the back of the subjects head far to one side of the screen. Either way is fine, but use at least a little bit of look space by putting the subject slightly off center and away from the direction they are looking.

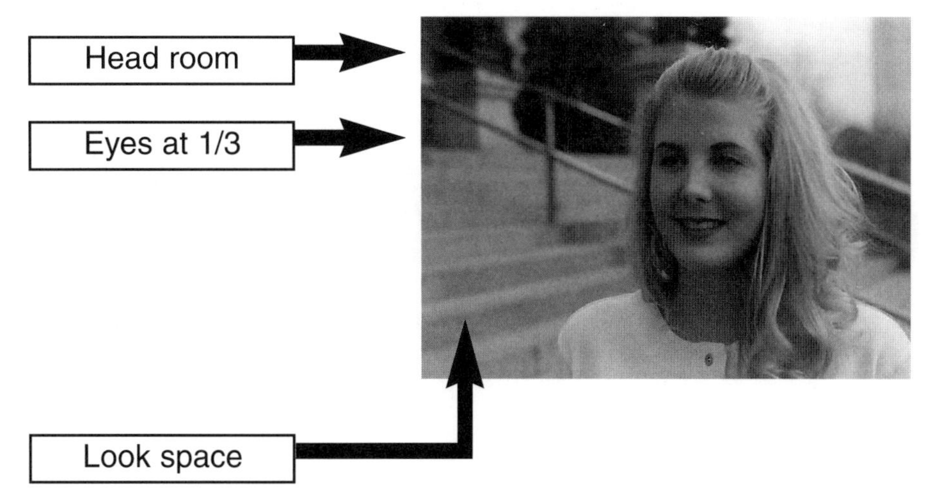

HEAD ON, PROFILE, 3/4 PROFILE

Which way is the person looking? Are they facing the camera? If so, that may be termed a *head-on* shot. If they are facing 90 degrees to the camera, then you see a *profile*. And if they are looking somewhere between a profile and a head on shot, and if you can see both eyes, then the shot is considered to be a *3/4 profile*.

Does it matter which head direction you use? Usually the type of production will determine head direction. For example, when you watch the nightly news, you expect the newscaster to face the camera, hence a head-on shot. It would look pretty silly to see the news anchor in a profile. On the other hand, if you see someone answering a question being asked by a reporter off camera, then the likely view is a profile or 3/4 profile.

Is there any advantage to using the 3/4 profile versus the profile?

The main advantage of the 3/4 profile is that it gives the viewer a better sense of the three-dimensionality of the face. It offers a partial side view and a partial front view.

Did you ever see someone for the first time in a profile? Until they turned their head toward you, you really didn't know what they looked like from the front. You could only imagine. Then they turned to face you and you couldn't help feeling surprised. You had imagined a different appearance.

Similarly, did you ever see someone at first from the front—head-on? Then, they turned to a profile and you couldn't help feeling surprised at the shape of their nose. It wasn't what you expected. The 3/4 profile alleviates these surprises by giving the viewer a three-dimensional sense of the subject's head.

Head-on

3/4 Profile

Profile

FRAMING TWO PEOPLE

Another common framing consists of two people in conversation. Interviews, for example, are one of the most commonly seen formats on television. Dramatic scenarios are also full of two-person conversations. So, what are your options for framing two people in a dialogue?

Option 1) Two profiles
The people face each other and the camera is perpendicular to them, catching both faces in the same frame, but both faces are in profile.

Option 2) Over-the-shoulder shot
Again, both people are facing each other. But in this case, the camera gets partially behind one person in order to see the back of that person's shoulder and a 3/4 profile of the second person. Keeping person #1's back of head and shoulder in the picture ensures that the viewer recognizes the relationship between the two people. The angle allows for an optimum view of person #2.

The problem is that only person #2 gets a favorable view. The solution is to switch angles and get an equal and opposite angle from behind the other person and alternate between the two shots. This second angle is called a *reverse angle.*

In a multi-camera situation, reverse angles are quick and easy because you have two cameras set up, one for each angle. Using the switcher, you simply select back and forth. But in single camera production, you must shoot one angle at a time and edit later.

Option 3) Two Faces East
Have you ever watched a soap opera and noticed both people looking in the same direction while talking to each other? Perhaps the woman, in disgust, goes to the window and stares out (facing the camera). Then the comforting boyfriend comes up behind her, also looking out the window. It seems a bit contrived, because we probably don't do that much in real life. But in the soaps or the movies it works nicely because it allows for something that the other two options cannot provide—two 3/4 profiles.

Two Profiles

Over-the-Shoulder

2 Faces East

THE DIRECTOR'S ROLE

The director must be familiar with all camera move options in order to choose the right move for a given scene. The director must decide whether a pan or a truck is to be used, whether a zoom or a dolly is best, or whether the camera should be static with no movement at all.

As director, your job is to know what you want to achieve, and communicate that to the camera operator. You may choose when to be specific about shot types and when to let the camera operator make his or her own choices.

Here are some examples of director's communication to the camera operator:

"Pan from left to right on a medium shot."
"Zoom in slowly from a cover shot to a close-up."
"Tilt up slowly from the desk to the person's face."
"Give me a static cover shot of the mountains. Hold that shot for about 15 seconds."
"Arc left from a medium shot of the drummer to a medium shot of the guitarist."
"Truck right from the man to the woman."
"Start with a close-up of the birthday girl. Wait about ten seconds and then dolly out to include the whole group."
"Go hand held and follow the man walking down the sidewalk."

In some cases, these moves may already have been specified in the script. But most of the time, the script will only describe a scene. The director will decide what kind of framing and what kind of movement the camera will make.

With the above examples in mind, consider what kind of moves and framings you will want your cameras to give you during any show you direct. Then, figure out the most concise way to note these directions on your script. You can go over your plans with your camera operators ahead of time. But also call the shots you want as you direct the live production.

CORRECTING SHOTS

A director should always keep an eye on the camera monitors to see what the camera operators are framing. Ideally, a camera operator will always frame a shot in an esthetically pleasing way. But the director must always be ready to make corrections as needed.

Look at each of the shots below. As director, what command would you give your camera operator to better frame each shot before you take to that camera on the air?

Correction?
a) pan right
b) pan left
c) tilt up
d) tilt down

Correction?
a) pan left & tilt up
b) zoom in & tilt up
c) tilt up & pan right
d) zoom in & pan left

Correction?
a) pan right
b) pan left
c) tilt up
d) tilt down

Correction?
a) pan right & tilt up
b) zoom in & tilt up
c) tilt down & pan right
d) tilt down & pan left

JUMP CUTS

Jump cuts are illogical or displeasing shot juxtapositions.They are most common in single-camera production where shots are taped out of sequence and then pieced together in the editing room, leaving room for logical sequencing errors. For example, in one scene, a man has a drink in his right hand. In the next cut, the drink instantly changed to the other hand. Or the clock on the wall suddenly changes time from one shot to another. These are simply the result of not paying attention to consistency while taping out of sequence.

Jump cuts like these are characterized by an illogical flow of action. But in live studio directing, illogical action flow is usually not a problem because there is no manipulation in the order of scenes. Live scenes, by definition, occur in real time and won't be vulnerable to the same kinds of mistakes.

However, live TV is not completely immune to jump cuts. There is another variety of jump cut that can plague the live director. This variety of jump cut is characterized by a displeasing juxtaposition of shots—a bad esthetic choice when transitioning from one camera shot to another.

Example #1 - Cutting between similar shots.
A cut from one shot to another in which the framing hardly changes looks very strange and senseless. To avoid this kind of jump cut, always vary the framing from one shot to another. Don't cut from a wide shot of the studio to another wide shot of the studio from a similar angle. Instead, cut from a wide shot to a medium shot, or from a medium to a close-up. By changing the framing, the director gives purpose to the shot change.

Example#2 - Cutting from A,B to B,C
Imagine that three people are sitting next to each other for an interview. If one camera frames person A & B and the other camera frames person B & C, the cut between the two cameras will shift person B from screen right to screen left in an instant, a strange and disconcerting visual experience.

Camera 1

Camera 2

Example #3 - Crossing the axis of action

Another version of displeasing juxtaposition is crossing the line that changes our directional orientation–*the axis of action.*

Imagine you are at a football game on the fifty-yard line. Your team has the ball and is moving down the field from your right to your left. As long as they have the ball, they should always be moving in the same direction from your point of view. Then, imagine the fans sitting across the field from you. They're on the fifty-yard line on the other side of the field watching the same action. But for them, the teams are moving from left to right. Either way is fine as long as it is consistent.

Now, imagine that you have just watched the first down. Just as the second down begins, you are instantly transported to the other side of the field. You quickly have to reorient yourself. Then you are transported back again for the third down. It would get annoying and confusing.

In the football example, the axis of action runs right down the field between you and the players. You can get up and walk around your side of the stadium, but as long as you stay on your side of the axis of action, your orientation stays the same.

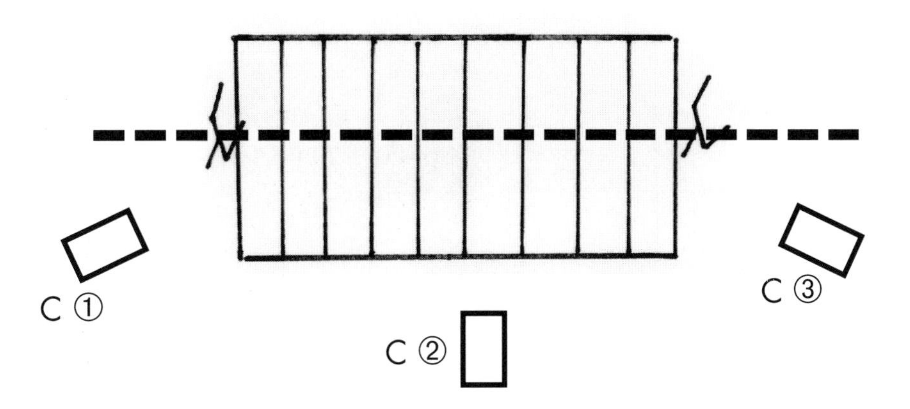

The axis of action is an imaginary line running the length of the football field. As long as you're on one side or the other, the direction of action stays consistent. Place all cameras on one side or the other. In any scene, consider where the axis of action runs.

Another example is in the theater. When an audience watches a performance on stage, the axis of action runs right along the front of the stage and separates the performers from the audience. You may be sitting down front on the far left side of the orchestra seating and someone else may be seated down front far right. You each see a different angle of the stage, but both of you are still on the same side of axis of action, so your overall orientation is the same.

Although a variety of camera angles may be used, they should stay on one side of an axis of action. When shooting scenes for television, be aware of the consequences of shooting one angle from one side of the axis of action, and the another angle from the other side. When you edit these shots together, you will have created a disconcerting series of cuts—a series of jump cuts.

In this set of over-the-shoulder shots, the cameras stay on one side of the axis of action. He looks screen right and she looks screen left. That makes logical sense.

In this set of over-the-shoulder shots, the cameras are on opposite sides of the axis of action. He looks screen left and so does she. That doesn't make sense, because in reality, they are looking in opposite directions.

A very common breach of the axis of action rule occurs in the taping of interviews. Let us imagine that one reporter is interviewing one guest. They are facing each other. The axis of action runs right through the two of them. As a director, you will want to shoot an over-the-shoulder shot and then a reverse angle. You can shoot from either side of the axis as long as you remain there for each angle. Otherwise, the orientation of the two people will change on the screen.

PUTTING IT ALL TOGETHER

Let's put it all together by covering a range of helpful tips. Some of these tips will apply to the more complicated upcoming exercises, so you may wish to refer back to this chapter from time to time.

Every control room has a different monitor arrangement. Get to know the monitors in your control room. Preview and line are usually color monitors. The rest are black & white.

CONTROL ROOM MONITORS

A multi-camera studio control room is full of TV monitors, sometimes dozens of them. At first, it can seem overwhelming. *Why so many monitors? Which ones do you look at and when?*

Each monitor is associated with a camera, VTR, or other video source. You look at the monitor to confirm proper picture before switching to that source in your program.

For example, how do you know what your camera operators are framing? Look at the camera monitors. How do you know if CG is typed and ready? Look at the CG monitor.

Imagine that you are directing a show and it's time to roll a commercial. How do you know whether the commercial is cued up and ready to go? You know because you check the monitor devoted to the VTR that has your commercial on it. You'll see the "3" of a countdown. Then, after you call for the VTR roll, you check the program monitor to see that the commercial is actually showing up on line when it should. If it doesn't, the TD may have made an error.

EXAMPLE OF TV CONTROL ROOM MONITOR CONFIGURATION

Line Monitor

Also called Program Monitor. This is the most important of all monitors. It shows you your actual program as it would go out over the air. Specifically, the line monitor looks at the output of the switcher. The switcher is the final stop for all video sources. It's where you make all your shot decisions. So, whatever comes out of the switcher is what goes out to the public—or out to your recording VTR. Whereas many of the control room monitors are black and white, the line monitor is always in color.

Air check monitor

This monitor is a tuner. In the event that your signal is actually going out over the air, this monitor tunes in the signal as it comes back from the transmitter. If you see your signal, you can rest assured that the surrounding community is seeing it as well. Thus, the line monitor only confirms that the signal went out of the studio, but the air check monitor confirms that the signal was broadcast.

Preview Monitor

The preview monitor is positioned next to the line monitor. It is used to take a sneak look at a source that may not be on line at the moment. Since most source monitors are in black and white, the director may wish to preview the given source in color. The TD may select any source on the switcher in a "preview" mode which shows up on the preview monitor.

Camera Monitors

Each camera in the studio has a corresponding monitor in the control room for the control room crew to see, usually in black and white. Source monitors are traditionally in black and white so as not to distract attention from the line monitor. The camera monitors should always be arranged from left to right, just as the cameras in the studio are arranged from left to right in numerical order. This helps the director understand the relationship between the cameras when viewing the monitors.

VTR Monitors

Each VTR has a monitor. They are usually numbered or lettered to correspond with the VTRs. For example, if there are two playback VTRs and one record VTR, they might be numbered VTR 1, VTR 2, and VTR 3.

MONITORS OR TUNERS?

In the TV business, there are TV sets that are monitors and TV sets that are tuners. It helps to understand the difference.

A TV tuner is like your set at home. It tunes in TV stations. The TV signal, which is broadcast through the air, is known as "RF" which stands for radio frequency. The RF signal is made up of: the video signal, the audio signal, and a carrier signal that transports the video and audio through the air. The TV tuner requires internal electronics to decode radio waves as they come down the antenna. The tuner in the TV must electronically strip off the carrier wave and separate the video and audio signals.

A TV monitor, on the other hand, does not require the tuning components. It simply accepts basic video and audio signals without any carrier. A monitor is typically receiving the direct output of a nearby video source: a camera, a VTR, an audio tape machine, or a CG, to name a few.

So, when you see a TV that has an input labeled "RF" or "antenna in," you know that the TV has a tuner and the input is made to accept an RF signal. When you see an input labeled "video in" or "audio in," you know that these are monitor inputs only, designed to take pure video or audio from some playback machine or camera and that this set will not tune in a TV station. Or, some sets do both.

CG Monitor

The CG operator will have a monitor for typing. There should also be a redundant monitor on the control room wall so the director can easily confirm that the correct CG is ready to go.

Two channel capability

Some graphics systems, such as CGs and digital effects computers, have two channel capabilities. That means they can carry on two separate functions at once. A two channel CG is a lot like having two CGs in one, each able to perform independently and each with its own output. Advantages of two channel systems are:

- the option for the operator to work on one file while another one is being used
- the ability to send sources to different places. One signal might be feeding the studio; another might feed an edit room.

Similarly, a two channel digital effects computer offers the advantage of layering effects from two different channels of graphics simultaneously.

Consequently, any two channel system will have two monitors, one for each of the channels. If the studio has a two channel CG, you might see two monitors side by side labeled CG-A and CG-B. Or, a two channel digital video effects computer output might be labeled DVE-1 and DVE-2.

HELPFUL HINTS FOR PLANNING AND SCRIPT-MARKING

1. Always use a pencil. You will definitely be erasing. If you use a pen, imagine the mess. Imagine the difficulty reading your own notations stained by blots of ink as you inevitably make corrections. In this age of high-tech graphic tools, the good old pencil is still your best friend when planning shots and marking scripts.

2. The beginning of the script on page 1 should begin at least halfway down the page to allow room for opening notes and reminders. What are the opening camera positions? What's the first preset effect? Which name ID comes up first? These and other notes are helpful to put at the top of page 1. Then, of course, you need to list all your opening ready commands. All this can easily take up half of a page. So if page 1 doesn't give you ample room on top, you may need an additional sheet for notes.

3. Make photocopies of your unmarked script for practice. Even with a pencil, you'll be making lots of changes and erasures, thus creating a messy script. Once things are pretty well decided, you can decide how easy your notes are to read. If things get a little too smudgy, you can transfer all your final decisions onto a nice clean original.

4. Draw an arrow from a command to the exact word in the script where a cue should occur. For example, if you want to roll VTR three seconds before the end of an announcement, then draw an arrow from the command "Roll VTR" to a word in the announce copy that appears three seconds before the end. That way, your eye can quickly follow along to the spot where the command should be given. As the announcement is read, you see exactly where and when to call for your VTR roll.

5. Write ready commands in left half of your notation column and enclose the readies in boxes; actual commands go on right half of the notation column. It's up to you whether to ready a command. In a new, unfamiliar situation, you should give more ready commands for a crew that doesn't know what's coming. In a familiar, repetitive situation like a daily newscast, the commands become fairly standard and expected. In that case, you may choose to minimize your list of ready commands..

6. Troubleshooting = visualizing. Use a floor plan to help visualize as you prepare. Create a little model studio out of cardboard. Make little stand-up figures to represent talent, cameras, and furniture. Play out your show like you were playing chess or checkers. Quickly, you'll see whether or not a camera move works, or whether the talent can get from position A to position B in the given time. Visualizing makes everything clear.

7 Circle camera numbers, for example Camera 2 is marked as ②. A circle distinguishes the camera number from any other number that may occur in your script. By circling, you don't have to write the word camera next to the number or even an abbreviation. The circle says it all.

8 Scripts must be amply spaced—at least double-spaced. You'll find out quickly that plenty of room on the page helps when writing lots of readies and commands. You may develop your own preferences for script formats. When it comes to VTR rolls, for example, you may want three or four lines of blank space to allow for the cluster of commands that occurs going in and out of each VTR segment.

9 When typing a script, paragraphs of spoken words should never be split across pages. Always end a paragraph on one page and start a new one on the next page. This format specification helps the director as well as the talent. The talent doesn't have to change pages in the middle of a sentence or a thought. The director can see the entire thought before turning the page.

USING REHEARSAL TIME

1 It's your turn to direct. Your studio time has commenced, at the end of which you must have a finished production. Right now, everyone is standing around waiting for you to take charge. What do you do? How do you grab the reins? Here are some steps you can take:

• Ask for all crew and talent to take their positions.

• Ask your AD to quickly take the crew list and make sure everyone is in the right position out in the studio.

• Meanwhile, you can go over instructions with the control room crew. Make sure the VTR operator has the right segment playback tape and that audio knows which music to play and which mics are being used.

• You may decide it's worth a minute to go out in the studio yourself and orient the talent and the camera operators. Don't take too long at this. You want to get the rehearsal going a.s.a.p. However, a minute or two to explain things to the studio crew may save confusion during run-throughs. You've been envisioning the studio setup during all your planning. The studio crew members don't know what you're thinking. So you want to quickly make sure that easels and furniture are where you want them, that cameras are placed according to plan, and that the talent knows where to look.

• Ideally, only a few minutes have transpired. Now you're back in the director's chair ready to begin a rehearsal. Do a quick confirmation that people are on headset. You don't want to begin barking commands if the intercom isn't working. Do a quick roll call. "Camera 1?" "Yes" "Camera 2?" "Here." This should only take a few seconds because you only have to call for those people you can't see. Those in the control room sitting right around you can hear and see you.

• It's easy to let time slip by. Figure out the most efficient way to get to this point, thus ensuring yourself the most rehearsal time before air time. Get your AD to help wherever possible. — *Now, you're ready!*

2 Go over presets so that everyone knows where to start.

• Prepare your TD by going over opening EFX. What is your first effect? Perhaps it is a CG name ID over ②. Note the opening effect on page 1 of your script and prepare the TD with the information, "Your first effect will be CG/②."

• Tell each camera what framing to begin with. *"Camera 2, start with a cover shot of the studio. Camera 1, you're on a head and shoulders of the talent. From there, you'll get the easel card."*

• Does the CG have the right title on line?

• Is the first VTR roll cued up?

3 Now, it's time to start a runthrough. A common mistake is to wait too long to begin a rehearsal. Don't wait until the top of the next minute. You don't need to have the AD do a lengthy countdown. You can begin a rehearsal almost immediately whenever you wish. Simply announce that the rehearsal is about to begin, say your readies, give your opening commands, and off you go.

Sometimes a short countdown is helpful for rehearsals. If you wish, have the AD give a 10-second countdown to give a sense of timing to the rehearsal. The goal is to get going quickly.

If you get off to a bad start, stay cool, call for a stop, regroup, and begin again. Don't waste time continuing if the opening falls apart. It's okay to freeze everyone and just take it over from the top. Quickly reestablish all your opening positions and cues and begin again.

If you're much further into the rehearsal and things disintegrate, you can stop everyone by saying "FREEZE." Then collect your thoughts and pick up right from where you left off. Don't worry about the clock. Stay cool. Try to get through everything once even if you have to stop and start. Remember, the rehearsal is your time to use however you wish. You make the strategy. Just try to be efficient and leave enough time to regroup before air time.

4 Try to accomplish one full run-through. After that, only rehearse the hard parts: transitions into and out of segments. Don't waste precious rehearsal time on easy parts such as talent reading a lengthy news segment. Stop everyone after a successful transition, find the next transition and say, "Okay, now let's go to the end of that segment and pick it up from the words, 'We'll be back in a minute with a look at...' Floor manager, does the talent know where to pick it up? OK. Ready roll VTR, ready dissolve VTR sound up. Q talent, roll VTR" With those words, you're on to the next segment.

You would not want to fully rehearse spontaneous interview segments. Instead, simply take the time to adjust your camera angles for good matching over-the-shoulder shots. Then rehearse opening and closing transitions. Get microphone checks on each talent.

If you can get through the body of the show at least once and the difficult transitions twice, you should be pretty well prepared. This assumes your rehearsal time is very tight. On the other hand, if you have time to spare, then of course, you can put more effort into fine tuning by rehearsing further.

5 A common mistake is to waste a lot of time adjusting audio levels instead of rehearsing. Instruct your audio person to adjust mic and music levels while you rehearse. Don't make everyone wait while the audio person fine tunes levels prior to rehearsal. If the music level isn't quite right at first, or if the talent mic is too loud or too soft, keep going. Chances are the audio person is making the correction. If, into the rehearsal, the levels still sound bad, then, it's time to take a moment and deal with it.

6 There will always be twenty-five things you could check or rehearse before air time. Typically, you'll only have time for a few of those things. Developing a sense about which few are important will make all the difference.

7 Pay attention to time-of-day during the rehearsal. You have an imminent air time coming up. The AD should keep you informed throughout the rehearsal time, "10 minutes to air, 7 minutes to air, etc." As the air time gets very close, the AD should be even more frequent, alerting you every thirty seconds or so. In the final minute, the AD should announce "1 minute to air," "45 seconds," "30 seconds," "20 seconds," and then give a ten second countdown, "10, 9, 8, 7, 6, 5, 4, 3, 2.." The AD can stop after 2. That's because the director should be giving a set of opening commands right at the 1-second mark and the two voices might compete.

GIVING COMMANDS

1 Start delivering your opening commands during the final second of the countdown to air—not after the countdown is completely finished—by then it's too late. It takes a second of time for a response by those you're speaking addressing. For example, at one second left, you can give opening commands such as, "Q MUS, F VTR." In the second that it takes for response, the timing should be just right.

2 Q TAL before taking or dissolving to talent, but do it in the same breath. "Q TAL, T②" rather than "T②, Q TAL." This allows for the normal reaction time for FM to cue TAL and avoids any "egg on face" as the talent's face appears on the screen not yet having seen the cue. It's a common mistake for new directors to allow too much lag time between the talent cue and the video transition. Practice saying them as if they were joined together.

3 Close the studio mics when going to tape, film, etc., to avoid recording unwanted sounds from TAL or studio crew. Write commands to close and open mics when appropriate.

4 Say "Ready" clearly so as not to confuse the crew with actual commands or you may get premature reactions. It's easy for a crew member to hear a mumbled ready, think it was the actual command, and act too soon. Make sure your crew understands the difference between a ready command and an actual command.

5 Know your script and commands as well as you can; try not to bury your nose in the script due to lack of familiarity with the material. Keep your eyes on the monitors as much as possible—that's where the action is.

The famous NBC symphony conductor Arturo Toscanini, among others, memorized all his scores and conducted every concert without having to look down at the music sheets. Similarly, a TV director who has studied a script at length could conceivably do the same. On the other hand, a nightly newscast has new elements making it unreasonable to memorize. Nonetheless, a director needs to watch the monitors as much as possible. Otherwise he or she may miss a glaring error as their nose stays buried in the paperwork. A new director will tend to look down at the script too much. But as the skills and familiarity set in, directing should become more connected to the monitors and less to the script.

Important times to look at monitors:

• After breaking a camera to a new scene, look up to make sure the camera actually got there and framed up properly before taking to that camera.

• When calling an actual transition command such as "T②," look up to confirm that the transition took place. Just because you said it, doesn't mean the TD actually pushed the button. You need to see for yourself in order to be truly in command.

6 Practice delivering commands until it becomes second nature. Practice at home. Practice using friends as TAL. Memorize sets of commonly delivered commands that get you in and out of typical situations such as program openings, commercials, SOT VTR rolls, etc.

7 Learn to scan all monitors including: source, preview and line. Don't direct just by looking at the line monitor, nor just by looking at the camera monitors. All are important. The black and white camera monitors are your guides to choosing the next shot. They also show you whether or not the camera operators have properly prepared the next shots for you. Thus, you are constantly checking the camera monitors. At the same time, the line monitor shows you what the TD actually selected. Your eyes are constantly searching back and forth from script to camera monitors to line monitor. Prior to VTR rolls and CG effects, you'll want to glance at those monitors as well, making sure that the right information is ready to go.

8 Be aware of scripted versus unscripted segments. In the course of a news show, you will transition from scripted segments where commands are all preset, to unscripted segments where you don't know exactly what's coming next. An unscripted segment may be an interview or a demonstration. In these cases, the talent is spontaneous and unrehearsed. Then, you have no choice but to carefully watch the camera monitors, evaluate what is about to happen, and call for the appropriate takes. Then, as the unscripted segment draws to a close, be aware of where you are in the script so you can get back on track.

9 Don't give crew impossible tasks, e.g. requiring a camera operator to move his or her camera across the studio faster than possible. In your preplanning, you have to imagine the speed at which a camera operator can move from one location to another. If you wait until the rehearsal period to discover that your expectations were unreasonable, you will waste a lot of time refiguring shot selection and commands.

10 Recording level versus monitor level. Don't confuse a loud monitor speaker with an audio signal that's turned up too high. The audio board usually has a monitor level adjustment which only affects the level at which you're hearing a speaker in the control room. It has nothing to do with the sound level going to tape. So, you must trust that the audio person is watching the meter for proper audio level, and if you as director wish to have the sound louder or softer in the control room, then simply request that the *sound monitor* be turned up or down, not the record level.

11 Avoid jump cuts. Review the kinds of jump cuts that can occur in live television and plan to avoid them. One type of jump cut is between similarly framed shots. For example, if you're taking from a wide shot of the talent to a close-up, that should work fine. However, you want the difference between the wide and the close to be substantial. Don't cut from a waist shot cut off at the belt to another waist shot cut off at the navel. Those shots are too similar and therefore disconcerting.

•Don't cross the axis of action. Keep your cameras on the same side of the action, just as all cameras need to stay on the same side of the football field so the ball always goes in the same direction.

•Don't cut among a group of three people so that a person who was on the left of the screen suddenly appears on the right.

13 When you tell a camera to move, be clear about the difference between smoothly executed hot moves on line and quickly breaking cameras to new locations once they are off line.

• If C① is on line and you want a slow zoom in, that's a hot move. The camera person should be aware of that.

• However, if you take to ②, which means you're off ①, and you instruct ① to "break" for the next shot, then that move is a fast relocation effort. No need for smooth movement. Just get there fast and be ready for the next take.

A good way to make things absolutely clear is by saying, "C①, you're hot, slowly zoom out and pan right to include the second guest." Or, you may say, "C①, break for the easel," in which case the operator will act as quickly as possible. You, as director, take responsibility for looking at the monitor to see that the camera is indeed off line before calling for the break. It is common for a director to accidentally call for the break while the camera is still on line. What an embarrassment!

14 When you cue up a VTR for a roll-in, you want a three-second pre-roll time to give the VTR a chance to lock up to speed. (With newer faster locking machines, the pre-roll time can be shorter. Check out the situation with the playback VTR in your control room.) A VTR roll occurs in three steps:

•First, cue to the right preroll spot on the tape. You want the "3" of the countdown leader showing on VTR monitor for verification. That assures you that the VTR is cued up three seconds prior to the roll-in. Or, if there is no countdown leader, just make sure that you are three seconds ahead of where you want to do a transition to the VTR.

• Second, you want the VTR operator to "ROLL VTR" on command, three seconds before you do your transition to the tape.

• Third, once the VTR has begun rolling, you wait two-three seconds, watching the VTR monitor for the countdown to end, then quickly call for the transition, executed by the TD. In this case, we want a dissolve, so the commands are: "ROLL VTR" at three seconds to the segment, then "✕ VTR," at one second remaining to transition to the segment.

15 Crew members—avoid the temptation to anticipate the director. Wait until you hear the command, even if you know it's coming. Sometimes the crew can jump the gun. For example, cameras have tally lights which indicate whether a camera is on line or not. When the light is on, the talent may start to speak, not because the FM gave a cue from the director, but simply because they saw the light. That can be a problem. What if the director had not intended for the TAL to start speaking yet? Perhaps the announcer was still talking. Similarly, a camera operator may base his or her decision to break according to the tally lights. That can also lead to trouble. The crew should assume that the director knows what he or she is doing and wait for verbal commands.

On the other hand, there are times when a crew member can tell that the director has clearly lost track of the situation. In this case, the crew member takes a risk and decides to anticipate what the director really meant to do. This is always a judgement call. It can backfire. At the same time, it can save a director from an embarrassing situation. Unless you, as crew, are sure you're doing the right thing by interpreting the situation, it's best to wait for the director's commands.

16 ADs: Don't out-shout your director. Help keep an orderly tone in the control room. Often, ADs and Directors are talking simultaneously. The AD may be giving a time cue while the director is calling a shot. This can be frustrating and confusing. It's up to the AD not to upstage the director. Wait a moment to give your time cue while the director finishes a set of commands.

17 In a classroom situation, the goal is to record the show for later review. It's a live-to-tape production. So, don't forget to give the first command, "Roll and Record your record VTR" or you won't have anything to watch later. Do this at least thirty seconds before air.

18 Always thank your talent and crew. After a tedious or strenuous production, take the time to personally go around the studio and thank the various individuals who obeyed your every command for the past hour.

After you've had some experience directing, refer back to these tips. You may gain a new appreciation for them.

Now it's time to move on to the script exercises. Each exercise is a lesson in itself and is accompanied by further instruction—each exercise will add several new challenges. The introduction to each exercise will explain the new challenges. Gradually, you will add skills and diversity to your directing of live studio-based programs.

Part II
Script Lessons and Exercises

THIRTEEN SCRIPT LESSONS & EXERCISES

Exercise 1 — Morning News Break *(simple newscast, one easel pic)*
Exercise 2 — Midday News Break *(theme music, picture change)*
Exercise 3 — Show and Tell *(unscripted demonstration)*
Exercise 4 — Top of the Morning *(variety, VTR roll-ins, camera moves)*
Exercise 5 — Afternoon Report *(news, backtimed, teaser, commercial)*
Exercise 6 — Business News Digest *(music deadroll, VTR SOT V/O)*
Exercise 7 — Eye on the Nation *(news, 2 anchors, V/O SOT V/O)*
Exercise 8 — High Tech *(demonstration, backtimed, multiple VTR rolls)*
Exercise 9 — Student Spotlight *(one-on-one interview)*
Exercise 10 — Movie Classics *(variety, scripted and unscripted, VTR rolls)*
Exercise 11 — Community Calendar *(2 guest interview, multiple VTR rolls)*
Exercise 12 — News Extra *(complex news format)*
Exercise 13 — Good Afternoon America *(complex variety format)*

The next part of this workbook features thirteen script exercises, each one adding levels of complexity. The formats include: news, demonstration, interview, and variety.

Prior to each new script is an orientation, explaining the new elements for each script and offering some pointers to head you in the right direction. Even if you do not use these scripts for actual in-studio productions, each exercise makes a good study opportunity—a chance to consider how you would handle each new situation, and a chance to practice script-marking and segment timing.

This book contains all thirteen scripts. However, to avoid writing in this book, please find all scripts and forms in the *Multi-Camera Director: Supplement*, a separate booklet. Besides the scripts, the *Supplement* contains one set of associated blank forms: floor plans, lighting plots, segment timing sheets, and crew lists. You may photocopy any or all contents of the *Supplement*. If you do not have a *Supplement*, your instructor may provide copies of scripts and forms.

Please note: in this book, you'll find the scripts printed double-sided like normal book pages. However, the *Supplement* provides the scripts in a standard single-sided format. You should always use single-sided script pages for actual directing. That allows you to lie pages flat on the console in front of you and helps you follow along without having to flip pages, which could very quickly leave you confused or lost.

The following exercises may call for easel graphics, VTR roll-in segments, and music themes. Your instructor has a media kit that contains these items. As director, you need to be familiar with any production elements ahead of time. So, look through a given script, see what graphic or VTR elements are required and take a look at them. For example, preview a VTR roll-in to identify the in and out cue and to verify the exact running time for your segment timing sheet.

Most of the scripts call for character generator titles. They may be required for opening and closing titles, name IDs, weather information, stock exchange figures, phone numbers, and more.

Be aware whether a CG, announce, or music theme is already integrated in a VTR roll-in, or whether you need to create the element yourself. For example, in one script, a VTR opener may not have a built-in announce, in which case you must cue your own live announcer over the VTR. However, in another case, the announce may be prerecorded into the VTR open. The only way you know for sure is to preview any VTR elements.

These exercises assume that your studio has the following equipment: two cameras, switcher, VTR playback, VTR record, character generator, audio mixer to handle at least two microphones, cassette playback for music, and intercom. If your studio is missing any of this equipment, you may modify the scripts to suit your facility. For example, you can use easel cards in place of a character generator for titles and name keys.

MORNING NEWS

GOALS

1. Students serve as crew while instructor or advanced student directs exercise #1, giving class a feel for the pacing and style of the director and the responsibilities of crew positions. The exercise is repeated while students rotate through each crew position.
2. Then, students direct the same exercise.
3. Suggestion: No air times at first and no grades. Make sure all students can easily handle the first exercise.

PROPS/MATERIALS

1. EASEL CARD: President and first lady

CONSIDERATIONS

1. Sometimes the art of TV directing can seem a bit abstract until seen in action. It would be equally hard to describe to someone how to conduct a symphony orchestra and then have them go on stage for the first time, never having seen the process before or never having played one of the instruments.

   Therefore, it's helpful if the instructor or advanced student demonstrates prior to the first exercise. In other words, the instructor actually directs a practice round over and over while each student rotates through the crew positions. This serves two purposes:

   - It allows the students to practice crew positions.

   - It enables students to feel what it's like when it all comes together before directing themselves..

2. There are some blanks in the script copy for you to fill in: the name of your talent and the station call letters your class chooses. Each director will have his or her own TAL, so each person's script will have a name change for the CG operator to type in.

3. The first exercise is very basic—no music, no camera moves. This script simply allows you to try some basic transitions, and develop the feel of cuing ANNC and TAL. Get a sense of the timing of transitions and how it works when you deliver the commands "Q TAL" followed by "✕①." Most of all, get a feel for how to use your rehearsal time effectively.

4 Your effects are: CG over switcher background color. If, for example, your CG is on button #5 on the switcher and the background colors are on button #7, then your effects are 5 over 7 or 5/7.

5 Note your opening shots and effects on top of Page 1 of your script. By writing these little reminders to yourself, you have a quick reference for where everyone should be at the outset of the show. You don't have to waste time recalling what C①'s opening shot is, for instance. This allows you to quickly get everything ready prior to each rehearsal or airtime. For this exercise, your opening shots are:

- C① - TAL HS (Head and Shoulders)
- C② - EASEL PIC
- EFX - CG/color background

6 A sample marked script of exercise #1 is in Appendix A. Your marked scripts do not have to look exactly like the sample, but you may find it helpful to compare.

7 To plan your production without having to write in this book, loose scripts and forms are found in the *Multi-Camera Director Supplement.* If you don't have the *Supplement,* ask your instructor for forms, or create your own. Permission is given to photocopy any item found in the *Supplement.*

AIRDATE/TIME ________________

CG - "MORNING NEWS AND WEATHER WITH

____________________________"

ANNC:

You're watching ________________.
(Station Call Letters)
the leader in up-to-the-minute news coverage. Time now for the Morning News and Weather with

______________________________.
(Name)

(DISSOLVE H/S TAL)

TAL:

Good morning. I'm ___________
and here are today's top stories.
In local news, a man is behind
bars tonight after a high
speed police chase through the
streets of the city. The man,
who has not yet been identified, is
suspected of having stolen more
than 100 automobiles in the area
over the past year. In national news,
the President and First Lady left
Washington today to vacation in
Martha's Vineyard.

(EASEL PIC #1 -
President/First Lady)

The President will be joined by the
Vice President. Their vacation is
expected to last ten days, although it
could be cut short, according to a
White House spokesperson. The
spokesperson told reporters today
that the President may find it necessary to spend extra time lobbying
legislators on his latest health care
reform package.

In international news, some Australians had a rude awakening this morning. A meteorite hit the township of Broken Hill in New South Wales last night, causing earthquake-like vibrations throughout the area. Hundreds of distressed residents called police saying they had seen a huge white light plummeting toward the ground. Police were not aware of the exact location of impact, but scientists confirmed it was a meteorite.

In sports, the Houston Rockets celebrate another NBA title as they beat the Orlando Magic in four straight games. This is the second national sports victory for the city of Houston and one that will not soon be forgotten.

Today's weather forecast looks fair and mild for the remainder of the day. Temperatures will drop to the mid 40s by midnight tonight. And tomorrow looks to be slightly cooler with a high of 68 degrees.

The week-long outlook calls for a warming trend by the middle of the week, followed by a chance of increasing wind and showers as a minor front moves across the state.

That's our up-date for this morning. Please tune in again for the Midday News for more top stories, sports and weather. I'm _____________, have a good morning.

CG - "MORNING NEWS AND WEATHER WITH _____________________________"

ANNC:
This has been the Morning News with _____________________________.
And you have been watching _____________-TV, your choice for news and information.

MIDDAY NEWS

NEW ELEMENTS

1. Introduce theme music
2. Change easel pix

PROPS/MATERIALS

1. THEME MUSIC
2. EASEL CARD: Marvin Williams
3. EASEL CARD: White House Spokesperson
4. EASEL CARD: NFL Quarterback

CONSIDERATIONS

1. In Exercise #1, you had only one easel graphic. Nothing had to be changed or moved. This time, you'll have three. You can't change them while the camera that's framing them is hot, so you need to coordinate off-camera changes.

   Even for a simple task such as changing EASEL PIX, the director must maintain responsibility for all commands. Nothing can be assumed. Therefore, the director must write in a command, something like "CHNG EASL PIC," to be directed at the FM or the Floor Assistant.

   Even though the crew will often know what's coming next, they should not do anything unless told by the director. In real life, a crew member will occasionally "save" a director by catching something that the director misses such as failing to change an easel graphic in time for the next shot. That may be fine at some later point. But for the sake of learning skills and refining the protocol, it is best to make the director responsible for all commands. For example, don't change the EASEL PIC unless told to do so. Once a director fails to call the command, then sees the wrong PIC on the monitor, the lesson will sink in quickly.

   In the professional world, it can be dangerous for a crew to assume that a director failed to give a command. A director may have done things a certain way intentionally. Knowing if and when it's okay to "save" a director can be tricky and should be discussed in a crew meeting so that the director has a chance to explain his or her view on the matter.

To change an EASEL PIC during a production, let's assume you have C② framing the EASEL. You want to change EASEL PIX while you are off C②. So you need to T①, which puts you back on the shot of the TAL. Then, your FM or FA can change the EASEL PIC while C② is off line. Once you see in your preview monitor that the new PIC is in place, take back to C② as soon as the script calls for the new graphic.

Your commands will be something like:

R①

T①

(to get off the Easel)

CHANGE PIC

(spoken *to the FM or FA—*
then look to see that it's been changed)

R②

T②

(gets you back to the Easel
with a new PIC)

It is important to realize that these graphics changes come at prescribed points in your script. The content of the scripted news story determines the timing of these camera takes. At the same time, you have some flexibility with exactly when to take back and forth.

2 In this script, you will introduce theme music at the open and close of the show. You can call "HIT MUS" for a full volume start, or "FADE IN MUS," or "SNK MUS IN." You can also have music go to background ("MUS BKND") in order to introduce a voice such as your ANNC over the level of the music.

When the announce is over, you can either swell music full again before fading it out, or just leave it at a background level while cuing the studio talent.

You may want to call for SNK MUS OUT just before cuing TAL so the music is already fading gradually while the TAL begins.

Your opening commands might look like this:

R F MUS
R F EFX
R O ANNC MIC
R Q ANNC

F MUS
F EFX

O ANNC MIC
MUS BKGND
Q ANNC

R O TAL MIC
R SNK MUS OUT
R Q TAL
R ✕1

O TAL MIC
SNK MUS OUT
Q TAL
✕ 1

Study the order of these commands within each grouping. It's best to put the music cue in your command sequence BEFORE your visual command. For example: "F MUS, F EFX," rather than "F EFX, F MUS." A picture on the screen with late sound looks more like a mistake than sound coming up a little before a picture.

3 To plan your production without having to write in this book, loose scripts and forms are found in the *Multi-Camera Director Supplement.* If you don't have the *Supplement,* ask your instructor for forms, or create your own. Permission is given to photocopy any item found in the *Supplement.*

AIRDATE/TIME ____________________

MUSIC

CG - "MIDDAY NEWS AND WEATHER WITH ________________________________"

ANNC: You're watching ______________________, the leader in up-to-the-minute news coverage. Time now for the Midday News and Weather with __________________________.

(DISSOLVE H/S TAL)

TAL:

Good afternoon, I'm ____________

and here are the headlines. Bail was posted today for the local man in jail following a high speed police chase through the city.

EASEL PIC - WILLIAMS

The man, now identified as 33-year old Marvin Williams, told reporters he was simply trying to get his wife to the hospital.

TAL H/S

Police are dismantling the car Williams was driving for possible hidden drugs. Williams, suspected of having stolen more than 100 automobiles in the metro area, is also believed to be responsible for a rash of other felony thefts.

In national news, the President's vacation was cut short today following urgent news from the White House.

EASEL PIC -
WHITE HOUSE ADVISOR

A White House advisor announced today that he was about to embark on a mission to free American hostages in Jakarta.

TAL H/S

Upon his return to Washington, the President informed the advisor that there are currently no known American hostages in Jakarta.

In sports, will he ever retire? Denver Broncos' Super-Bowl-winning quarterback John Elway just can't seem to leave the game.

EASEL PIC - ELWAY

Even though he announced his retirement, rumor are flying that the "pushing 40" quarterback may come back for more. Neither Elway's trainer nor his manager could be reached for comment.

TAL H/S

Besides being the oldest, Elway has been the highest paid quarterback in the NFL.

Today's weather forecast continues to look fair and mild for the remainder of the day. Temperatures will drop to the low 40s overnight. And tomorrow looks to be warm and sunny here in the metro area.

That's our up-date for this afternoon. Please join us again at five for the afternoon report.
I'm ___________________________,
Have a good day.

ANNC:
This has been the Midday News & Weather with
____________________.

And you have been watching ______________-TV, your choice for news and information.

MUSIC

TITLE

SHOW AND TELL

NEW ELEMENTS

1. To direct an unscripted exercise
2. To learn to watch monitors and react to what's happening in the studio

PROPS/MATERIALS

1. Each student picks something to demonstrate. The item could be anything from a camera to a tennis racket. The class can decide whether the TAL or the DIR is responsible for picking the item to demonstrate.
2. THEME MUSIC

CONSIDERATIONS

1. The program has a scripted open and close. But once you get past the opening music and announce to your TAL, the rest is unscripted until it's time to close.

2. Your goal here is to use two cameras to capture an unscripted demonstration. You'll want to have the cameras close to each other—one camera on a wide shot or a waist shot of your TAL, the other on a close-up of whatever he or she is demonstrating. You may take back and forth to these cameras at will. No need to mark your script with these takes. Just watch the monitors and call R ①, T ①, R ②, T ② as you see fit. This exercise will give you a chance to concentrate on what the TAL is saying and call for the appropriate takes. When the TAL is explaining a concept, for example, you may take to the camera that frames the waist shot of the TAL. When the TAL refers to the item in hand or on the table, you may take to the close-up camera, and so on throughout the presentation.

3. Although you don't have to back time this show to the minute, you should agree on a time at which the FM will show a wrap sign. The TAL should then gracefully bring the demonstration to a close. ADs can start to pay attention to time. The AD can be assigned to watch for a clock time that is two or three minutes into the show. At that time, the AD may tell the FM over the headset to show a wrap sign. This technique puts only moderate pressure on the director to keep track of time, yet ensures that each exercise runs approximately the same length of time. Suggestion: The show should be about three or four minutes.

4. The script calls for a wide shot of the studio at the outset. You may want to instruct your TAL to look busy until he or she is cued to welcome the audience. That means your second camera should be ready on a waist shot to receive the TAL's welcome. Once you have taken or dissolved to your second camera on the waist shot, you can break the first camera to a close-up of the demonstration item and wait for the TAL's first reference to the item that would suggest cutting to the close-up.

5 How to handle rehearsal. In this exercise, you do not need to rehearse everything. Why bother? Since your TAL is speaking off the cuff, it will never come out the same way twice. So what's important to rehearse? Openings, closings, transitions, and anything else that you should know about the demonstration. For example, if the TAL plans to ignite a chemical reaction on the table, you should be aware of when and how it's going to happen. You may want to be prepared with a wider camera angle.

So, in your rehearsal, walk through the motions, but don't necessarily have your TAL perform the whole routine. Directors, communicate with your TAL. Have them tell you what they're going to do. Establish a clear understanding about how much you can accomplish in a short presentation. Cover something simple like how to load a film camera, as opposed to how to rebuild an engine.

Cameras close for demonstration—similar angle of view.

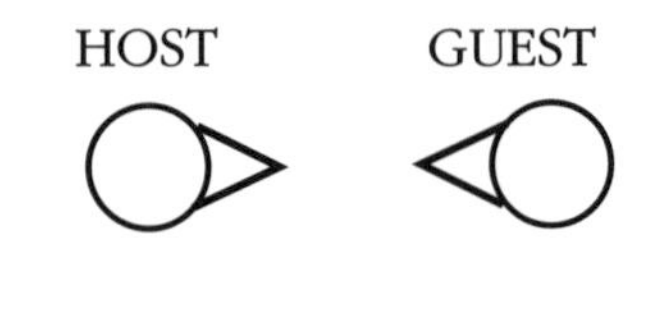

Cameras fanned out for interview cross angles.

6 Since you're going to use one of your cameras for a close-up of something that the TAL is demonstrating, you'll need to think about camera positions. Should the cameras be next to each other? Should they be spread out wide? Does it matter?

Do you recall how late night talk show hosts like Johnny Carson would show graphic cards to the camera? They held them way off to the side so that some camera off in another part of the studio could get the shot.

Ideally, you don't want to have to hold something off to the side. It looks more natural to have the host hold the item in roughly the same direction he or she is looking. So, for any demonstration situation where you want to cut back and forth between a shot of the TAL and a CU of whatever he or she is showing or demonstrating, it is ideal to have your cameras close and parallel—representing the same point of view.

On the other hand, in an interview situation, as you will be doing later, you want just the opposite. There you want cross angles achieved by having the cameras fanned out for opposing over-the-shoulder shots.

Either way, cameras should always stay in the same relationship to each other, from left to right, the same as your monitors in the control room. In other words, don't have C② cross over the wires of C① to pick up something on the left side of the studio. This left-to-right consistency eliminates a lot of confusion, not to mention tangled camera cables.

7 To plan your production without having to write in this book, loose scripts and forms are found in the *Multi-Camera Director Supplement.* If you don't have the *Supplement,* ask your instructor for forms, or create your own. Permission is given to photocopy any item found in the *Supplement.*

AIRDATE/TIME ________________

OPENING MUSIC ON TAPE

C① ON WIDE SHOT OF STUDIO-
TAL LOOKS BUSY

KEY TITLE OVER C①

ANNC: Welcome to Show and Tell, where every day, we learn something new. Today, our guest host is ____________, who will be showing us __________________________.

DISSOLVE TO C② ON WAIST
SHOT OF TAL
TAL WELCOME

DEMONSTRATION

CLOSE:
TAL SIGN OFF

SNEAK MUSIC

DISSOLVE TO WIDE SHOT

KEY TITLE OVER C①

ANNC: Thank you for joining us for another edition of Show and Tell. Please join us again next week right here on this station.

TOP OF THE MORNING

NEW ELEMENTS:

1. Instead of news, this will be more of a variety show format *a la* Good Morning America.
2. Now, you'll start keying CG over video tape *and* changing CG pages during the show. You'll need a CG page for the program title, and another CG page for the Food Fest Hotline phone number.
3. In the first two exercises, cameras did not have to move. Now, C② will break from TAL to EASEL and back at least twice during the show.

PROPS / MATERIALS:

1. VTR WITH MUSIC FOR OPEN/CLOSE
2. TAL PROP: Bob Smith print
3. EASEL CARD: Carolyn Jones letter
4. TAL PROP: Food Fest tickets
5. EASEL CARD: Lana's poem

CONSIDERATIONS:

1. Just as in Exercise #3, when you direct a demonstration, place your cameras near each other so that close-ups and cover shots look like they are from the same angle.

2. Heads up while directing.

   By now, you should feel somewhat comfortable with directing. It's time to check in with yourself and see if you're on your way to being a "heads-up" director.

   For most beginning directors, the hard part is paying attention to what's going on around you while you're learning to give commands from your script. Besides looking at your script, you have to look up to watch all your monitors just as you did in Exercise #3.

   Watch your camera monitors to see whether cameras are framing the proper shots before you call for them. You don't want to take to a camera while it is still focusing or moving. You should glance at VTR to see if it's cued up before calling for a VTR roll. You should glance at the CG monitor to see if the right page is up. And, you also need to glance at your line monitor to see whether your TD is switching properly. For example, when you call for a dissolve, the line monitor is where you will actually see the dissolve occur as it is executed on the switcher.

A director should look at both camera monitors and line monitor. If you only look at the camera monitors, you may not notice whether the proper camera is actually on line. Similarly, if you only look at the line monitor, you don't know whether the cameras are framing shots properly.

The DIR is able to keep an eye on the monitors.

The ultimate goal is to have your head up as often as possible. Don't bury yourself in your script while directing or you'll never see what's actually on your monitors. Try to be familiar enough with your script and your commands that you do more "glancing" at and less "reading" of the script. This will come with time and practice.

It's not easy to follow a script and keep glancing at monitors, but you will learn to sense the right times to do each while the show is under way. The AD can help follow along in the script.

It's a great idea to practice at home. Perhaps you can have a friend read the ANNC and TALENT copy while you "learn your lines," practicing your commands and getting intimately familiar with your script.

Remember that "Truth" is whatever appears on your line monitor. That's what's going out to the world in the live broadcast. It's possible to give all the right commands and yet have a line monitor that, for some reason, is in black. Even though you're saying all the right things, the TD may have goofed. Maybe you called for a take to C① and the take never actually happened. In order to be in control, you have to look up and see what's going on.

3 This is the second script using music. In case you didn't try this last time, you can tell your audio person to swell music after the closing announce. In other words, after you say, "MUS BKGND, CUE ANNC", wait for the announce to finish. Then say,"SWELL MUS." Bring it all to a close with FSAPO.

4 This is your first videotape roll. Now you can regard VTR as another video source on the switcher, and the audio tracks of your VTR should appear as another audio source on the audio mixer.

In some cases, the videotape roll has to be absolutely precise in order to hit a particular start point, such as the beginning of a commercial. However, in some cases the video roll does not have a hard and fast starting point. For example, if the video is simply supplying you with generic shots of traffic for your traffic report, then it may not be so crucial where you make your transition.

In this exercise, you won't have to worry about a precise start point for the VTR. The important thing is to have the videotape rolling ahead of time so that the tape is up to speed before you do your transition. The VTR shows a city scene that can be faded to at anytime. Be aware of how much tape you have remaining so it doesn't run out midstream.

Videotape segments are referred to in a variety of ways: "tape," "VTR," "roll-in," or "package." *Package* refers to a self-contained field story from a field reporter for a newscast.

Videotape roll-ins can be MOS, SOT or a combination of the two. MOS means "No sound on tape." It stems from a humorous take-off on the German, "Mit Out Sound." SOT has a more sensible translation: "Sound on Tape."

MOS tape is usually used in a situation where the news anchor continues to read while the DIR simply rolls tape and cuts to it. A script may indicate VTR MOS V/O, meaning that this tape roll-in will be voiced-over by the TAL.

You will be seeing combinations of SOT and MOS later in the exercises. It's essential to know whether your tape is MOS or SOT. Audio needs to know as well. That's because VTR audio goes through the audio mixer. The TD controls the picture portion; AUD controls the sound portion.

If VTR is strictly MOS, AUD has no concern. But if there is any SOT, then AUD must be sure to check the proper fader on the audio board and check sound level on the tape.

In this case, the videotape contains your music—that's for efficiency, so you don't have to use yet another source for your music. You can learn to regard the video portion of the VTR as separate from the audio portion—you can fade the music and the picture in and out independently of each other. For example, you can roll VTR with sound down, and then call for the music when you want it along with the video fade up.

Your opening commands might go like this:

R ROLL VTR
R F VTR, SND UP
R ✂ EFX (title/VTR)

ROLL VTR (Roll it several seconds before your show starts.)
F VTR, SND UP (This command comes just before the end of
✂ EFX your countdown, to allow for reaction time.)

R O TAL MIC
R SNK MUS OUT
R Q TAL
R ✂ ①

O TAL MIC
SNK MUS OUT
Q TAL
✂ ①

Re-Q VTR (For close)

Roll the VTR again at anytime during the TAL's closing story. Make sure you know how much videotape there is. In this case, you have a full minute of the city scene.

5 You have two EASEL PICS, the letter from Carolyn Jones and Lana's poem. You shouldn't need to move C② but you will have to break C② to get the EASEL PIC. Here's how it will work: Once you're done with C② on the CU of the Bob Smith painting, then say "C② break for EASEL PIC." Make sure you look at C②'s monitor and see that the camera is ready on the Carolyn Jones letter before you take back. When you're off C②, break it back to get the CU of the Food Fest tickets in the TAL's hands.

6 You can position the TAL behind a desk, or on a stool, or sitting on the front of the desk in a casual manner.

7 Since this is not news, but a more personalized variety show, the talent should not be just reading off a script but should establish some eye contact with the viewer. You can use teleprompter system or make cue cards. One set serves the entire class. A third option, is to have the TAL hold the script in one hand and read from it, looking to the camera as often as possible to establish eye contact. The TAL can use the other hand to hold up the items called for in the script.

8 To plan your production without having to write in this book, loose scripts and forms are found in the *Multi-Camera Director Supplement.* If you don't have the *Supplement,* ask your instructor for forms, or create your own. Permission is given to photocopy any item found in the *Supplement.*

9 Appendix B shows you a sample marked script for this exercise.

AIRDATE/TIME__________

VTR SOT (THEME MUSIC)

TITLE:

CG/VTR "Top of the Morning with

________________."

ANNC:

You're watching __________-TV.

Time now for Top Of The Morning,

with your host

_____________________________.

HOST:

Hello, and welcome to Top of the Morning. Today, we've got some fun things in store for you. We've got some suggestions for what to do around town this weekend. We've got some weather updates. And, to start off, did you know about this weekend's benefit art auction at the Circle Gallery? I'd like to show you one of the prints by Bob Smith that will be up for auction.

TAL SHOWS PRINT

TAL AD LIBS A BRIEF

DESCRIPTION OF THE PRINT

They wouldn't give us the original. That's because the original is pretty valuable. This is a reproduction of "Stardust," one of only a few original works by the popular Bob Smith.

Sixty percent of the proceeds from the sale will go to the Children's Hospital Oncology Fund. Bidding for Stardust will start at $5,000. You won't want to miss out on the chance to bid. For more information, call the Circle Gallery at 551-5151.

Next, we have viewer mail, a regular segment on Top Of The Morning. Today's letter comes from Carolyn Jones of Bend, Oregon who writes:

CU EASEL PIC - LETTER

"Why do you continually promote the works of Canadian artist Bob Smith on your program? There are plenty of other artists of much greater talent than this fake. Why don't you feature sculptor Bob Jones of Bend, Oregon? Thank you sincerely, Carolyn Jones, Bend, Oregon."

We'll get our producers on it right away.

What to do this weekend besides visiting the Circle Gallery? It's time for the yearly Food Fest at Civic Center Park which opens Friday morning and runs all weekend. Admission is free, but you'll need to buy these.

SHOW CU - TAL HOLDS TICKETS

Food tickets are available all around the park at the reasonable price of 5 for $10. These tickets are redeemable at any food concession. If you've never been to the Food Fest before, this is a good time to get out and see how much fun it is.

CG - FOOD FEST INFO HOTLINE
555-FOOD

Call the Food Fest Hotline for a full list of restaurants and entertainment.

Let's take a look at weather and see what the weekend has in store. The outlook for today is continued sunshine. More of the same tomorrow. Sunny and dry. And the weather experts tell us to expect the trend to continue for the rest of the week. Good news for Food Fest or for anything else you plan to do this weekend.

And finally, today—remember our elementary school poetry contest? Well we have the winning poem from this year's competition in the 2nd grade category. Before I read this, I just want you to get a look at it—we gave her extra points for her fabulous handwriting.

EASEL PIC - POEM

AD LIB ABOUT NEAT HANDWRITING

Her name is Lana Davis. She is only 9 years old and a 2nd grader at Skyline Elementary.
And here is her poem.

"If stars can be together in the sky
Then why can't we stand side by side?
If stars can twinkle so bright
Then why can't we, instead of fight.
Stars are peaceful and nice to see.
That's what we should try to be."

Thank you, Lana, for your poem. You deserved to win and we look forward to seeing many more poems from you in the future.

That's it for today. Thanks for joining me for Top Of The Morning. I'm your host, ____________________, wishing you a pleasant day.

ANNC:
You've been watching Top Of The Morning, with ___________________. Stay tuned for the Afternoon Report, here on ______________-TV, your best source for news, sports, and weather.

AFTERNOON REPORT

NEW ELEMENTS:

1. Precise program length
2. VTR Commercial
3. Teaser

PROPS/MATERIALS:

1. EASEL CARD: Bank building
2. VTR MOS: Escape from bank
3. VTR 1:00 COMMERCIAL BREAK
4. EASEL CARD: Gregorian Chants CD
5. EASEL CARD: Tommy Moe

CONSIDERATIONS:

1. *Backtiming* - You are required to end this show at a precise time. In TV, form is often more important than content. In other words, it is more important to be out on time than anything else. So, since timing is more important than your script, the script may be changed to accommodate time. Before you resort to shortening or lengthening the script, you might simply see if the TAL can speed up or slow down a touch to keep the show on time. But you're certainly free to cut or add to the script. The best situation is when you have a little extra time. Don't worry about adding copy. Just extend the closing by stretching out the music and delaying the ANNC cue.

   Directors, make sure your ADs understand the segment timing sheet. You are relying on them for updates along the way and a final countdown to get you out on time.

   The DIR should rely on the AD to count down the first and last ten seconds of the show so that the DIR doesn't have to watch the clock.

> ADs—remember, your job is to help the director keep track of time amidst a flurry of activity. Think about how you are most useful. Don't distract the director or try to compete with him or her. If the director is in the middle of a sequence of commands, wait a moment, but then make sure he or she is aware of time. Above all, make sure you are on track with the final seconds of the show, counting down the final ten to fifteen seconds so that the director can end on time.

2 TEASER - Many shows use a *teaser* segment at the outset of the show. That means the host or anchor appears before any opening titles to give a sneak preview of what's to come. That teaser segues to either a commercial followed by the opening of the show, or to the opening of the show itself. Some of the remaining scripts will begin with teasers.

3 COMMERCIAL - This time, your VTR roll must be precise, since the commercial has a definite starting point. You must dissolve just before the very beginning of the commercial—no sooner, no later.

You begin with the "3" of the countdown leader showing on your monitor, which tells you that the VTR is cued three seconds prior to the commercial. About two seconds to the end of TAL copy you say "Roll VTR"; then at the end of copy, say "✕ VTR SOUND UP."

Make sure you kill TAL mics during the commercial. Then, near the end of the commercial, open your TAL mics again, and listen to the AD's countdown as you prepare to "Q TAL and ✕ ①" which gets you out of the commercial and back to the studio.

4 There are two ways to prepare the front end of a VTR segment to accommodate the director's "roll" cue. One way uses a countdown leader. The numbers count down until they reach the number two. During the remaining countdown time, the screen is black. Thus, you have two seconds of black before the segment starts. It is during those two seconds of black that you call the transition—usually a dissolve.

If the countdown leader went all the way to one second, you might see the number "1" on the screen during your dissolve. If you roll the VTR with "3" left to go at the point where your TAL is about 2 seconds from the end, that means you will have about a second of black on your VTR in which to do your dissolve. If you roll your VTR too early, your commercial will have started already. If you roll too late, then instead of a tightly timed transition, you'll be sitting on your TAL waiting for the countdown to get past the "2."

If you're going to err one way or the other, it's best to roll VTR a touch late. Sitting on your TAL for an extra second is better than cutting into your commercial midstream.

Some other tricks to make your transition work well are: plan to dissolve to a wide shot of the studio or a title graphic for a few seconds before going to the commercial. This transition, called a *bumper*, serves to get you off the TAL CU for the few seconds it takes to roll the VTR, thus avoiding the so called "egg on face" as the TAL sits there wondering if you're off or not. If you feel comfortable trying it, your commands would look something like this:

R ✕ C② on CS R ROLL VTR R ✕ VTR SND UP

(C① is on a CU of TAL.)
(C② is on a cover shot.)

✕ ②
ROLL VTR

✕ VTR SND UP (2 seconds later)
KILL TAL MIC

Whatever you do, keep an eye on the VTR monitor so you can see when the commercial leader gets past the two and into black. Then you're safe to call for your dissolve. If you're not looking, you may be dissolving into the leader numbers.

5 Use the time during the commercial to check segment timing. Once you're into the commercial, you can relax for a few seconds and check in with the AD. The AD should be aware of whether you got into the commercial late, on time, or early. If you got in more than five or ten seconds late, you may want to speed the TAL up a bit on the other side. If you got in early, you can either slow the TAL or plan on a stretched MUS close. If it is only a couple of seconds off, don't worry. Use your FM to communicate any instructions to the TAL during the commercial, if necessary.

It's important not to confuse ideal time with real time on the commercial. The ideal time may have been to start the commercial at 4:01:00; the real time may be 4:01:05. You must first note what time the commercial *actually* began and count from there in order to get out of the commercial right on time.

6 ADs: During the commercial, give the DIR a :30 warning, a :15 sec warning and a 10 second countdown to the end of the commercial. The DIR has a lot to think about. The AD can help by keeping the DIR apprised of remaining time.

7 It's very helpful to know the *outcue* of the commercial or of any VTR roll-in segment. For example, if the final words of the commercial are: "Call for your free booklet today," then those words should either be marked in the script, or the AD should remind the DIR that these are the last words, in addition to giving the countdown. The commercial or other segment may end with music instead of voice. Then, the outcue may be described musically instead of verbally. For example, the out-cue may be referred to as: "MUS FADE" or "MUS FINALE."

8 Here's a point about segment timing that often confuses people: Getting into a particular segment late or early does not necessarily throw off the rest of your segment timing sheet unless you're off by a huge amount. If you get into the commercial a few seconds late or early, don't try to rework all your other numbers. Just acknowledge that one of the following segments will start a bit early or late and will be longer or shorter. But don't try to rewrite numbers on the segment timing sheet. Simply let the following segment or segments absorb the difference.

Some segments have a certain amount of built-in flexibility; others do not. The more tightly scripted a segment, the less flexible it is. So, you may need to think ahead a segment or two in order to figure out where to make up the time, if necessary.

Let's say, for example, that your commercial began five seconds late. You should still backtime the next segment using the same numbers on your segment timing sheet. The only difference is that you will anticipate getting to that next segment five seconds late. Perhaps you can make up the time during the course of that segment by speeding the talent, catching up five seconds and ending the segment at its prescribed time. Or, you might acknowledge that the segment is too tightly scripted to make up the time, so you allow it to simply begin and end five seconds late and look ahead to the following segment to make up the difference.

On the other hand, if you get way behind, you might need to cut a story or plan to cancel the announce at the end, or whatever you estimate will make up the difference. There again, you don't have to rewrite the numbers. If you throw out a story, then you assume that the segment containing that story will come out at the originally prescribed time as a result of the deletion.

9 To plan your production without having to write in this book, loose scripts and forms are found in the *Multi-Camera Director Supplement.* If you don't have the *Supplement,* ask your instructor for forms, or create your own. Permission is given to photocopy any item found in the *Supplement.*

Here's an example of a timing problem: During a commercial, you find that you should have gotten into that commercial ten seconds sooner—in other words, you're running ten seconds behind. You see that you have two more segments remaining: a news segment and a closing segment. The news segment is tightly scripted. The close has some room to play with. You can do a couple of things: During the commercial, have the FM instruct the TAL to speed up just a bit during the final segment. That should make up part of the time.

The rest can be made up during the close by simply spending less time swelling the music and ending shortly after the ANNC is finished. Or, if you're really running behind, forego the announce completely. The viewers won't know that they've missed anything.

ADs, it's a great idea to study a segment timing sheet and imagine different scenarios happening in the course of the show that throw off the time. How would you respond? Once you're used to thinking this way, you'll be a big help to your DIR.

AIRDATE/TIME ________________

TAL: (TEASER)

Two armed women robbed a down-town bank of more than one million dollars this afternoon. Police are in pursuit. I'm ________________.
I'll have details on this and other sto-ries along with traffic and weather in a moment.

OPEN: MUSIC

TITLE: CG/STUDIO COVER SHOT

"The Afternoon Report with ______________________."

ANNC:

You're watching _______-TV, the leader in up-to-the minute news. Now here's ________________.

TAL:

Good afternoon. Here are today's headlines.

EASEL PIC - Bank Building

In what is being called the Thelma and Louisecape, the downtown branch of Midwest Savings Bank was robbed just hours ago by two women. The women made off with more than one million dollars in cash. No one was hurt in the incident.

VTR MOS - Escape

And our news room has just obtained a home video tape shot by someone just outside the bank showing the escape of the unmasked duo. At the moment, the footage is being studied by forensic experts for identification of the two bank robbers. Anyone having information regarding this incident is asked to call metro police.

A $10,000 cash reward has been offered by the bank for help leading to the arrest of the two women. We'll play the videotape again on our evening and late evening news.

We'll be back with national news and weather after the following important messages.

COMMERCIAL 1:00

TAL: In national news, Wall Street reported record activity as the Dow Jones Industrial Average reached a record high—almost 100 points above the previous record high. Financial guru Louis Rukeyser attributes the gain to a steadily improving economy and a balancing of the foreign trade deficit.

Gold and silver prices were down today, as is often the case when the Dow rises. Gold sank $37 an ounce and silver $20 an ounce.

And here's a bit of interesting news in the worlds of business and entertainment. Dateline Madrid, Spain. Two former Benedictine monks who say they scored the music on a hot-selling CD of Gregorian chants, claim they are entitled to $5 million in royalties.

CU OF DISK - EASEL GRAPHIC

The 2-disk CD entitled "The Best of Gregorian Chants," unexpectedly soared to the top of the Spanish music charts and then gained worldwide sales of more than $3 million.

Music company officials claim the chants are public domain and are not protected by copyright. They also say that such chants cannot be scored or arranged, as the monks claim they did, because these are simply songs that have been sung seven times a day for hundreds of years.

EASEL PIC - Tommy Moe

Turning now to sports, Olympic Gold Medalist Tommy Moe surprised reporters at a press conference today when he announced that he will be preparing for the next Winter Olympics after all.

A few weeks earlier, the two-time medal winning ski champ said he was not planning to appear at the next Winter Games for personal reasons. However, that apparently has changed. Moe will be training near his home in Anchorage, Alaska. Look for Moe to appear on this winter's World Cup circuit as well.

Traffic in the metro area is pretty smooth and trouble free at this hour. No major accidents to report. We'll have a more detailed traffic report from the Traffic Watch copter during our next report at five o'clock.

In weather, temperatures are falling gradually as a cool air mass envelopes the region. We can expect lows tonight in the 30s and a possible record low tomorrow of 29 degrees. There you have it for this afternoon. Thank you for joining us. I'm

___________________.

Have a pleasant day.

CLOSE

MUSIC

TITLE: CG/STUDIO COVER SHOT

ANNC:

You've been watching the Afternoon Report with _______________.

Please join us again later today for the Evening News, here on __________-TV, the city's leader in up-to-the-minute news and information.

NIGHTLY BUSINESS DIGEST

NEW ELEMENTS

1. Music deadroll at end
2. SOT V/O
3. lower third ID
4. Two commercials, each :30

PROPS/MATERIALS

1. MUSIC AUDIO TAPE FOR OPEN/CLOSE
2. :30 COMMERCIAL BREAK
3. :30 COMMERCIAL BREAK
4. VTR SOT PACKAGE: Gateway Computers

CONSIDERATIONS

1. How do you time things so that a cut of music ends naturally just as you fade to black?
   Answer: By doing a *music deadroll.*

   Any time you roll a tape without actually using it on line right away, it's called a deadroll. The tape is rolling, but is not being incorporated into the show—yet! It's a trick for achieving precise timing at the end of a segment.

   In this exercise you will use a music deadroll on audiotape. Here, you want the music to end exactly when the show ends. In other words, you don't just want to fade out the music, you want the music to hit its final chord right at the end of the show.

   For example: Thirty seconds of music rolled thirty seconds prior to the end of the show—music that ends right on time.

   The strategy is this: Since you don't know exactly when to transition to the music because you don't know precisely when the TAL is finished talking, you set the music in motion ahead of time, properly timed to the end of the show. A one-minute cut of music is deadrolled exactly one minute before the desired end of the program. The timing remains accurate and the music is available anytime you wish to fade it up. Whenever the news anchor is finished, call for AUD to fade in your music and it should end on time.

   In fact, if the music deadroll begins on time, it now becomes a measuring rod for the end of the show. Listening for the music to end should be just as accurate as listening to your AD counting down the last seconds of the show. You can use the final chord of the music as a signal to FSAPO.

So, how to execute a music deadroll? In this exercise, you'll have a cassette full of one-minute music cuts. Have the audio person cue any cut to the beginning. Look at your segment timing sheet. What time does the show end? 3:00? Then your deadroll time is 2:00. The AD may assist the DIR by calling for the deadroll. He or she can even count down the last few seconds to the deadroll. At about 1:45, the AD can say to AUD: "15 seconds to deadroll." At 2:55 the AD can say "Deadroll in 5,4,3,2,1, DEADROLL MUSIC." Audio confirms, "MUSIC DEADROLL."

2 SOT, V/O - In this show, you will be rolling a VTR that has SOT on the first part for an interview bite, then MOS footage following for the anchor to voice over. You can take back to the anchor any time before that footage runs out.

Example of commands for an SOT, V/O:

R ROLL VTR R T VTR SND UP

ROLL VTR (three seconds before the point it occurs.)

T VTR SND UP (When the TAL finishes his or her line prior to VTR.)

R Q TAL

Q TAL (When the Sound Bite is over and it is time for TAL V/O. VTR is now MOS We hear the TAL and see the VTR on line.)

R ①

T ① (to go back to the TAL before VTR runs out.)

3 Lower third ID - You will be keying the TAL's name over the TAL's picture. That means your effects will be CG/C①. You must make sure TD sets up these effects ahead of time.

You can state your commands in one of three ways: You can either say: ✕ EFX, followed a few seconds later by LOSE EFX. Or, you can say ✕ EFX, followed by ✕ ①. Or KEY IN. KEY OUT.

This concept is sometimes confusing. The TD is moving the fader bar on the switcher from C① to a preset effect of CG over C①. Even though you're leaving the C① button and coming back to it a few seconds later, C① is still on the line monitor because it is part of the preset effect of CG over ①. In other words, you're really dissolving from C① to C①, but adding the CG in the context of the preset effect. On the screen, it looks as if nothing has changed except the addition of the title key. But on the switcher it means actually dissolving away from C① to the combine effect and then back again when you're finished with the effect.

4 Two commercials. This should be no different than rolling one commercial except that these are only :30, so you have little time to collect your thoughts. You now have two different commercials, giving you two separate checkpoints along the way, with time to confer with the AD on time and make modifications as needed. Remember to have the VTR operator recue for the next segment as soon as one if finished.

5 To plan your production without having to write in this book, loose scripts and forms are found in the *Multi-Camera Director Supplement.* If you don't have the *Supplement,* ask your instructor for forms, or create your own. Permission is given to photocopy any item found in the *Supplement.*

AIRDATE/TIME ________________

WIDE SHOT OF STUDIO

TEASER

ANCHOR:

Business news, financial news, product news—It's all right here on the Nightly Business Digest—next.

MUSIC

TITLE: CG/EASEL PIC OR CG/VTR

"Nightly Business Digest, with ________________________."

ANNC:

You're watching ________-TV, the city's leader in news and weather coverage. Time now for Nightly Business Digest with __________________.

TAL H/S

ANCHOR:

Hello, I'm _______________. Anti-smoking laws just got tougher thanks to a new federal law. The Dow Jones took a dive today. And Gateway Computers introduces a new affordable handbook computer. I'll have details on these and other stories here on the Nightly Business Digest right after this message.

COMMERCIAL :30

ANCHOR: (NAME KEY)
A ruling that gives retail businesses and restaurants much more freedom to deny smokers access was made today in a New Jersey circuit court. A group of citizens sued Burrito Bob's restaurant chain for failing to provide a smoking section. The judge found in favor of the restaurant.

In the opinion of the court, the restaurant is not obligated to provide smoking sections, citing health risks to other patrons of the establishment. The judge commented that providing a smoking section does not constitute meeting a basic customer need. This ruling sets the scene for many other businesses across the country to follow suit.

On Wall Street, the Dow took a tumble this morning, dropping 125 points. Experts differ on the reasons. Some point to seasonal profit taking as a key reason and see nothing to be alarmed about. Others say it is caused by a negative reaction by investors to international financial news. Reports indicate that the dollar is still dropping in relation to the Japanese Yen.

Reports indicate that international investing is up more than 28% whereas investments in US companies have leveled off this month.

Next up, a look at a handy new handbook computer by the mailorder master of the computer world—Gateway. That and more when the Nightly Business Digest continues.

COMMERCIAL :30

ANCHOR:
In our next story, we look at the quickly growing world of portable computers: laptops, handbooks, palmtops, and even smaller. Recently our consumer specialist, Peter Ziskin, took a look at a small yet powerful computer from Gateway 2000.

VTR - SOT - PACKAGE "Gateway"

VTR LENGTH: ____________

OUTCUE: I'm consumer specialist, Peter Ziskin.

ANCHOR:

And this latest news just came in—Gateway has announced a three-for-one stock split effective next month. And Merrill Lynch just upgraded the company's rating from a "buy" to a "strong buy" which should trigger an increase in the stock price over the next few days.

That's our look at the world of business for tonight. We thank you for joining us. Please, tune in again tomorrow. Good night.

CLOSE:

MUSIC

STUDIO COVER SHOT

CG TITLE

ANNC:

You've been watching the Nightly Business Digest. Stay tuned for MASH next, followed by I Love Lucy—here on your news and entertainment channel.

EYE ON THE NATION

NEW ELEMENTS

1. Two TAL
2. Key info over TAL shoulder
3. V/O SOT V/O

PROPS/MATERIALS

1. EASEL CARD: City Skyline
2. VTR OPEN/MUSIC/:30 COMMERCIAL
3. EASEL CARD: New airport
4. EASEL CARD: Planes
5. EASEL CARD: Old airport
6. VTR V/O SOT V/O: Light Rail
7. MUSIC AUDIO TAPE: Bumper music
8. 1:00 COMMERCIAL BREAK
9. VTR CLOSE WITH MUSIC

CONSIDERATIONS

1. In this exercise, the VTR open has self-contained music and titles. You bring MUS to BKGND and cue the live ANNC.

2. TAL #1 will be the anchor. TAL #2 will be the weather person.

3. In this exercise, you'll be keying CG weather information over the shoulder of TAL #2. The trick here will be coordinating with your camera operators to pan on command, putting more room over the TAL's shoulder, while you're dissolving EFX of CG over a camera. Then, when you lose your EFX, you can have the camera center the TAL again. You'll want to figure out a well-timed command delivery that makes this move look smooth.

4. A *bumper* is a brief transition period when leaving the studio to go to a commercial. A familiar use of a bumper is the transition to a commercial during a late night talk show. After the host says, "We'll be right back," the band plays for five seconds or so while you see a program logo on the screen.

   Why have bumpers? Though not necessary, they create a little breathing space for the director to roll a commercial, or they allow the program to flash up teaser information such as: "What's coming up next?" You may add such a teaser CG if you feel inclined. In this exercise, a bumper can be as simple as dissolving to a wide shot of the studio while you fade up some theme music. Then roll your commercial and dissolve to it.

5 V/O SOT V/O - In this case, the anchor reads a V/O over the first part of a VTR roll. Then, the roll contains SOT. FInally, the VTR roll finishes with another V/O by the anchor. This is one step more complicated than your previous SOT, V/O, because the TAL must time the read accurately for the first V/O. If the TAL runs long, he or she will cut into the SOT. Better to err on the side of having the TAL end a bit early.

So, your commands might go like this:

Ready	Command
R ROLL VTR R T VTR SND DWN	
	T VTR SND DWN (TAL reads V/O)
R VTR SND UP	
	VTR SND UP (TAL waits for cue)
R Q TAL	
	Q TAL (TAL reads second V/O)
R ①	
	T ① (Take back to TAL on line before VTR runs out)

6 To plan your production without having to write in this book, loose scripts and forms are found in the *Multi-Camera Director Supplement.* If you don't have the *Supplement,* ask your instructor for forms, or create your own. Permission is given to photocopy any item found in the *Supplement.*

AIRDATE/TIME ________________

STATION ID: CG Call Letters over
EASEL GRAPHIC

ANNC:
You're watching __________-TV, the city's leader in news, weather, sports and information.

STUDIO 2-SHT
ANCHOR #1: A new international airport for the metro areas.

ANCHOR #2: And heavy rain is in the forecast. I'm _______________ .

ANCHOR # 1:
And I'm _________________. Join us for Eye on the Nation, next!

VTR OPEN / COMMERCIAL :30

SNEAK MUSIC OUT AND
DISSOLVE TO H/S TAL #1

ANCHOR#1
Hello and welcome to Eye on the Nation. Our first story highlights the opening of the new International Airport. It promises to become one of the busiest and most technically advanced aviation centers in the United States.

EASEL PIC - NEW AIRPORT

After failed attempts to open the 4.2 billion dollar airport by last Christmas of, the official opening occurs this week, hosted by the mayor.

The $200 million automated baggage system, which was plagued with operational glitches, now seems to work fine.

EASEL PIC - PLANES

The new airport's chief customer is United Airlines, which has contributed large amounts of money to the construction of the new facility. United will claim most of the B concourse.

EASEL PIC - OLD AIRPORT

Meanwhile, no one has decided what to do with the old International Airport near downtown.

Ideas have ranged from making it into a general aviation airport to turning it into a business park. Most likely, the acreage from the old airport grounds will be redeveloped into residential neighborhoods to accommodate the city's rapidly growing population.

VTR - V/O SOT V/O

V/O: (SHOTS OF NEW AIRPORT)
The new airport has some of the newest technology of any airport in the world with the ability to land planes in almost any weather.

(VTR CONTINUES WITH SCENES OF LIGHT RAIL)

And a light rail is being constructed that runs from downtown Denver to the new airport about ten miles away.

SOT: (CONTRACTOR DESCRIBES LIGHT RAIL)
outcue:__________ time:________

ANCHOR #2 V/O: The first section of the light rail will be finished next month. Then, contractors will work on the extension that takes metro area passengers from downtown to the new International Airport.

ANCHOR #1:
In financial news, the Dow Jones Industrial Average worried investors today by dropping 100 points. The drop came as a surprise during a week that has historically been a high one for the Dow. Analysts with Dean Witter Brokerage attribute the drop to poor earnings for some of the biggest Blue Chips including United Airlines and IBM.

We'll recap some of the day's biggest winners and losers tonight on the Business Update portion of the eleven o'clock news. In a moment, we'll have weather, but first, a word from one of our sponsors.

STUDIO WIDE SHOT
BUMPER MUSIC

COMMERCIAL #2 1:00

STUDIO WIDE SHOT
BUMPER MUSIC

ANCHOR #2
Here's a look at the weather. The forecast calls for rain.

CG/OVER SHOULDER
Rain Tonight
Daytime High - 53
Nighttime Low - 35

We can expect two to three inches of rain as a cold front heads for the city. That front should reach us within the next couple of hours. Daytime highs probably won't exceed 53 degrees and the nighttime low of 35 could include rain turning to light snow by midnight, unless of course that system moves on before the temperatures drop.

That's it for weather. More updates during our 11:00 news. And that's our report for today. I'm

______________________.

ANCHOR #1

And I'm ______________________.

Thanks for joining us. Tune in again tomorrow for Eye On The Nation.

CLOSE:

VTR/MUSIC/TITLE

LIVE ANNC:

You have been watching Eye On The Nation with ______________________

and______________________. Stay tuned for Star Trek, next.

HIGH TECH

NEW ELEMENT

1. To direct another unscripted demonstration. This one is timed.

PROPS/MATERIALS

1. Student provides prop(s) to demonstrate.
2. VTR OPEN WITH MUSIC/ANNC
3. :30 COMMERCIAL BREAK
4. VTR CLOSE WITH MUSIC/ANNC

CONSIDERATIONS

1. This demonstration format will have some scripted portions, but will be largely ad lib. Therefore, this script will be a form of a rundown, listing segments and key questions instead of full dialogue.

   So how do I handle this kind of format? Is it totally different?

   No. Your commands work similarly, so you can mark your script the same way in the open, close, and at transitions.

   One big difference, however, is that an unscripted program requires the help of your in-studio TAL. Your host or anchor must see time cues and wrap up his or her free-form segment on time. It's no longer good enough for the counting to be only among the AD and DIR. Now, the DIR and AD deliver time cues to the FM who, in turn, delivers them to the TAL. If you don't do this, your host might go on and on and your unscripted segment would never end!

   A good host will follow the cues accurately and wrap up a segment on time. However no free-form segment can ever be expected to get out right on the second, so you need to have flexible segments that follow in order to take up any slack. For example, if you leave room for a :20 close, and the host goes five seconds long, you can make the close into a :15 segment by fading out right after the ANNC instead of swelling the music.

   Try deadrolling your closing VTR. Choose an overall end time for your show and backtime the length of the close VTR to establish a VTR deadroll time. Be aware that the closing announce is already on tape. You need to have your host end in time for the announce.

2 During an unscripted segment, it does not make sense to write all the readies and takes on your script. Once a demonstration has begun, your eyes are on the monitors, watching what the TAL is doing. When you feel it's appropriate, you call R①, T①, etc. For example, when you hear the TAL say, "Looking closely you can see that..." you can respond by cutting to a close-up of what the TAL is showing. You might say: "②, break for a CU of the gadget." Then, as soon as the shot is focused, you call R②, T②.

3 In this exercise, students will find their own props to demonstrate as talent. Since the show is called High Tech, choose suitable technical gadgets to demonstrate. Some possibilities might be: a laptop computer, a lab experiment, a fax modem, a game, a tool, an electronic musical instrument, etc.

4 There is no scripted welcome by the host. Either write one or let your host ad lib.

5 To plan your production without having to write in this book, loose scripts and forms are found in the *Multi-Camera Director Supplement.* If you don't have the *Supplement,* ask your instructor for forms, or create your own. Permission is given to photocopy any item found in the *Supplement.*

AIRDATE/TIME ________________

SEGMENT 1 (length:________)

VTR/SOT: ANNC,MUS, TITLE

annc outcue: ...fascinating stuff."

SEGMENT 2 (length:________)

HOST:

WELCOME / DEMONSTRATION

SEGMENT 3 (length:________)

COMMERCIAL :30

SEGMENT 4 (length:________)

CONTINUE DEMONSTRATION

SEGMENT 5 (length:________)

CLOSE: STUDIO WIDE SHOT

VTR: MUSIC/ANNC/MUSIC

VTR deadroll time:_________

annc outcue: ".. today's technological world."

STUDENT SPOTLIGHT

NEW ELEMENT

1. Direct a one-on-one interview

PROPS/MATERIALS

1. VTR OPEN WITH MUSIC
2. 1:00 COMMERCIAL BREAK
3. VTR CLOSE WITH MUSIC

CONSIDERATIONS

Interviews require some new strategies:

1. Obviously, the interviewee is not going to read or memorize a script, but rather, will converse spontaneously. Thus there will be segments of the show where you have nothing to follow in your script. Instead you are watching the monitors and taking back and forth as your host and guest converse.

   By watching the faces on your camera monitors, you will know when a guest is about to respond or when an interviewer is about to jump in with a new question. Try to anticipate and take *before* either host or guest begin to talk, rather than always playing catch-up with late takes.

2. Camera angles become an issue now, too. Instead of parallel cameras that you used in news and demonstrations, you will want to shoot reverse angles of your host and guest. Interview angles are often called *cross angles*.

3. Floor managers must position themselves near the host's camera to give time signals and cues to the host. Unless the FM stays close to the host camera, the host will be forced to glance away in order to pick up time cues. Positioned properly, you allow the host to subtly see cues without looking away.

Cross angles for interview format.

FM stands near the host's camera.

Floor managers sometimes make the mistake of standing too far back alongside the host camera, afraid they will be in the camera's field of view. The problem is that they end up back in the shadows and are hard for the host to see. Try standing as far out in front of the camera as possible, near the front of the camera lens. You won't block the camera at all, but the TAL will see you clearly.

4 ADs can help the director with time cues to the floor in one of two ways: either the AD gives a time cue to the director who in turn gives it to the FM who in turn shows it to the TAL. Or, provided you have extra headsets for the AD, the AD can call times directly to the FM: "Show one minute," "Show thirty seconds," "Show wrap," "Show cut" at their designated times from the segment timing sheet. The FM responds by signalling the host using hand signals or cards.

5 Hosts—You'll be developing a feel for how to wind down an interview segment in the final minute. Be tactful in getting your guest to wind down. The easy way is to just say, "We only have thirty seconds left, can you tell me in one sentence..." A classier way to handle the wind down is to ask the kind of questions in the final minute that can be answered in short order and gracefully wrapped up. Practice will help tremendously. But there is always the unknown—every guest has a different style and personality. That adds to the challenge and the excitement. Throw in a little bit of intuition and a dash of good fortune, and your segment should end on time.

6 FINAL QUESTION—One technique for ending an interview is to have a *final question* or *key question* all ready to go: "So, tell us where to call for tickets," or "What do you think will be the outcome?" As the segment gets down to the minute, the host can go to this final question. This helps wrap up the discussion smoothly and on time.

Directors, you might decide on a final question with the host. Pencil that question in the script and, if time is running low, the host can go to that. Try to avoid the gimmick, "We only have thirty seconds left" or "We're out of time"—even if Ted Koppel uses it, it can sound crass.

7 The final segment must be out on time, but prior segments don't have to be so precise. For example, let's imagine you have a two-segment interview split by a commercial. If the first segment runs a little long or short, there's no need to take drastic action. Just collect yourself during the commercial, assess the time, and, if appropriate, apprise the host that the next segment may need to be a bit longer or shorter. Again, don't change the times on the segment timing sheet, just play catch-up.

You may have gotten into the next segment late, but you still abide by the times for that segment, showing 2,1,:30,W,C cues at their normal times—the overall segment is simply shorter because you started it late.

8 MATCHING OS SHOTS—Now, you're cutting back and forth between two people having a face to face conversation. Your choices are: over-the-shoulder shots or close-ups. Either way, try to balance the look of opposing shots. An over-the-shoulder (OS) shot from one direction should be about the same angle and field of view as the opposing shot. Look at your two shots on your preview monitors and adjust one camera or the other so that the framing looks equal and balanced. Use your rehearsal time to match OS shots.

9 To plan your production without having to write in this book, loose scripts and forms are found in the *Multi-Camera Director Supplement.* If you don't have the *Supplement,* ask your instructor for forms, or create your own. Permission is given to photocopy any item found in the *Supplement.*

Matching OS shots

Matching CUs

AIRDATE/TIME ________________

OPEN:

VTR/SOT: MUS, ANNC, TITLE

ANNC:

Up next—Student Spotlight, the program that puts you in touch with the lifestyles and personalities of today's students. And now, here's your host...

HOST:

Hello, I'm __________________.

Welcome to Student Spotlight, where we talk to people on campus who are doing interesting things in academics, sports, and politics. Today our guest is ____________ .

INTERVIEW SEGMENT

COMMERCIAL 1:00

HOST:

Welcome back to Student Spotlight,

as we continue talking with our guest

________________ .

INTERVIEW SEGMENT

Key Q:______________________

HOST CLOSE TO CAMERA

CLOSE:

VTR/MUSIC/ANNC ON TAPE

"You've been watching Student

Spotlight. Stay tuned for news—next."

MOVIE CLASSICS

NEW ELEMENT

1. A combination scripted/unscripted variety program.

PROPS/MATERIALS

1. VTR OPEN/MUSIC/:30 COMMERCIAL
2. VTR SOT: Good Guys, Bad Guys
3. VTR SOT: Modern Good Guys
4. 1:00 COMMERCIAL BREAK
5. VTR CLOSE WITH MUSIC/ANNC

CONSIDERATIONS

1. There are several VTR rolls in this show. The supplied VTR roll-in tape has all roll-ins lined up close together so that your VTR operator can recue each segment quickly. You decide which leader number you want showing each time. Three seconds is typical but you can do a second more or less depending on your playback VTR's capability.

   For your first movie clip, the roll-in contains two SOT segments, separated by a brief return to the studio. The host's bridge between segments is so short, a few seconds have been allotted in between so that you can just keep the VTR rolling. You'll want to practice this part for timing. Also, remember that there is a pad at the end of the first clip and the beginning of the second so if you get out of one late or into one early, you'll still have a picture on the screen.

2. The second half of your show has another interview segment, so you'll be going from a scripted to an unscripted segment.

   Unscripted segments offer certain advantages to the multi-camera director. You can spend more time looking up from your script, watching your monitors, and calling your shots as you pay close attention to the spontaneous flow of the conversation. Also, you can make up time during these segments. If you happen to get into a segment late, you can still end it on time.

3. In this program, the guest movie expert will be played by a fellow student as part of the rotation. When students are playing make-believe roles, it's easy to make a joke out of it. You must decide beforehand whether your intent is to be straight or comical, and convey that to your crew. This is another good opportunity to make a set of cue cards for the class to share.

4 To plan your production without having to write in this book, loose scripts and forms are found in the *Multi-Camera Director Supplement.* If you don't have the *Supplement,* ask your instructor for forms, or create your own. Permission is given to photocopy any item found in the *Supplement.*

AIRDATE/TIME ________________

TEASER

HOST:

Hello and welcome to Movie Classics.
Tonight, we'll be looking at action
heroes. And a little bit later,
we'll be joined by a guest movie critic
for insights into some of today's top
box office hits. Don't go away!

VTR OPEN SEGMENT

ANNC/MUSIC/ COMMERCIAL

HOST:

Hello, and welcome to Movie Classics. Later in the show, we'll talk about some of the current movies that are on the road to becoming classics with a guest critic from the New York Times. But first, we're going to begin with our traditional look at great moments in the cinema. Have you ever thought about why you don't see the good guys wearing white any-more? Remember the old cowboy movies? The bad guys wore black hats. The good guys wore white.

VTR - SOT: "Good Guys, Bad Guys"

HOST:

You don't see scenes like that in west-erns or police detective shows any more. Today, the good guys don't look all that different from the bad guys.

SAME CLIP STILL ROLLING

HOST:
In past decades, TV heroes from Superman to Sam Spade usually cooperated with the authorities. They were tough, but they played by the rules. The 1960s were years when much of the American public called something into question—authority. And that questioning of authority carried over into the movies. The establishment was not always right—even the police chiefs and the mayors. And the in-the-trenches good guys often had to rebuke their superiors in order to get the job done. In the streets, they did whatever they had to do, even if that meant taking the law into their own hands.

VTR - SOT: Modern Good Guys

HOST:

Today's heroes often snub their superiors and take law into their own hands—Steven Segal and Sylvester Stallone, to name just a few. When the establishment does not back them up, they forge ahead anyway and do whatever it takes to get the bad guy. The irony is that now the bad guy doesn't look much different from the good guy.

We'll be back in a moment to get some insights about why the good guys don't wear white anymore when Movie Classics continues.

COMMERCIAL

INTERVIEW SEGMENT (1-3 min.)

HOST:

We're happy now to welcome

_____________________, a movie

critic from the New York Times.

HOST ASKS GUEST ABOUT THE EVOLUTION OF GOOD AND EVIL IN MOVIES

HOST: THANK GUEST

Thank you for joining me for this week's edition of Movie Classics. Please join me again next time when we look at this year's Oscar nominees.

VTR CLOSE: MUSIC/ANNC

"You've been watching Movie Classics. Stay tuned for Community Calendar."

COMMUNITY CALENDAR

NEW ELEMENT

1. A two-guest interview

PROPS/MATERIALS

1. VTR OPEN WITH MUSIC
2. :30 COMMERCIAL
3. VTR CLOSE

CONSIDERATIONS

1. Now, you get to deal with two guests interviewed by one host. Camera set-ups are similar to the one-guest interview. Here, you have the option to go to close-ups of individual guests or stay on a two-shot or three shot OS. Suggestions include:

   ■ Start with a CU of the Host to introduce the show.

   ■ As the host introduces the two guests, take to an OS three-shot to establish the guests in relationship to each other and the host as seen in the photo below.

   ■ You can zoom in on whichever guest is answering the question.

   ■ You can anticipate who is going to answer the next question and break your camera to get on the H/S shot and be ready to take it when the guest begins to answer.

Host and guests positioned for a two-person interview.

2 Here again, students can play the roles of guests representing community agencies, arts groups, etc. Or you may bring in real guests.

3 To plan your production without having to write in this book, loose scripts and forms are found in the *Multi-Camera Director Supplement.* If you don't have the *Supplement,* ask your instructor for forms, or create your own. Permission is given to photocopy any item found in the *Supplement.*

AIRDATE/TIME ________________

OPEN:

VTR/SOT: TITLES,MUSIC,ANNC

"It's time for Community Calendar.

Now, here's your host."

HOST:

Hello, and welcome to Community Calendar.

INTRODUCE TOPIC

INTRODUCE BOTH GUESTS

SEGMENT 1

HOST AD LIBS TRANSITION TO COMMERCIAL

COMMERCIAL :30

SEGMENT 2

CLOSE:

VTR: VIDEO/TITLES/MUSIC

ANNC: "You've been watching Community Calendar. Stay tuned for News Extra."

NEWS EXTRA

NEW ELEMENT

A more complex news show requiring a variety of skills:

1. Package
2. V/O SOT V/O
3. Interview
4. Commercials

PROPS/MATERIALS

1. VTR OPEN WITH MUSIC/ANNC/:30 COMMERCIAL
2. VTR MOS: Boeing 777
3. VTR PACKAGE: Western Stock Show
4. 1:00 COMMERCIAL BREAK
5. :30 COMMERCIAL BREAK
6. VTR CLOSE WITH MUSIC/ANNC

CONSIDERATIONS

1. A *news package* is a prepared news report, edited on tape and ready for playback in the middle of the newscast. Sometimes CGs are already edited into the taped report. Usually, however, they are added during live newscasts. That's the way it is in this script. You must have a CG ready to title the interview bite during the package. You must know ahead of time when the bite comes and how much time you have to put up the CG.

2. After your second commercial, Anchor #2 interviews the mayoral candidate, played by a person from class. Decide how people will be seated. Does the interviewee take the seat of Anchor #1 during a commercial? Or does the interviewee sit to the other side of Anchor #2?

3. Going into the third commercial, your anchor has just finished an interview and is now going to "throw to a commercial" as the script says. In other words, there is no scripted segue. Your anchor must simply ad lib a transition, or you may work one out with him or her. You may want to use a bumper.

4. When your anchors have quick exchanges, you may decide whether or not to cut back and forth between close-ups of the host and guest or whether you see them both on a two-shot. Obviously the two-shot is easier, and there may be times when individual close-ups may be too much to ask of your camera operators, given the short time intervals. You decide which works best.

6 Announces are already on the VTR segments.

7 To plan your production without having to write in this book, loose scripts and forms are found in the *Multi-Camera Director Supplement.* If you don't have the *Supplement,* ask your instructor for forms, or create your own. Permission is given to photocopy any item found in the *Supplement.*

AIRDATE/TIME ________________

TEASER

ANCHOR # 1:

Hello, I'm ________________. In a moment, I'll have the headlines in today's national and local news.

ANCHOR #2:

And I'm ____________________.

I'll be interviewing our city's challenger for the mayor's office. Please join us for News Extra.

OPEN: VTR/MUS/ANNC/COMM

ANCHOR #1:

Hello, and thanks for joining us on News Extra.

VTR/MOS - BOEING 777

length:____

In national headlines, the Boeing company announced the successful test flight of its new 777 aircraft, the first fully computer designed airplane in Boeing's history. The plane is close to the size of a 747, but uses only two jet engines and is more automated and fuel efficient than any commercial aircraft to date. Boeing says it has orders to provide 57 aircraft to companies around the world. United Airlines has ordered 12 of the new 777s and Asian countries have ordered more than 30.

ANCHOR #2

And on the local scene, today marks the beginning of the national western rodeo and stock show.

PACKAGE :45

Outcue: ____________________

ANCHOR # 2:

It's been a mayoral race that some have called nasty. And it's down to two people, the mayor and his foremost opponent who is my guest here in the studio. We'll hear his/her ideas for the city and how he/she plans to beat the incumbent and what he/she would do about various problems that affect our city if he/she were elected. All this and more when News Extra continues after these important messages.

COMMERCIAL 1:00

ANCHOR # 2
INTRODUCE MAYORAL
CHALLENGER

INTERVIEW (1-2 min.)

THANK MAYORAL
CHALLENGER AT END
THROW TO COMMERCIAL.

COMMERCIAL :30

ANCHOR # 1:
And finally, the news you've been waiting to hear—a cooling trend. This heat wave that has caused terrible water shortages and fire danger in the hills is finally coming to an end. Temperatures will drop and rain is actually in sight as a cold front moves our way tonight and should pass through completely by morning.

The following twenty-four hour period should see 1/4 to 1/2 inch of rain in the city. Much needed.

ANCHOR #1: (AGREES)
(TO CAMERA)
That's our news for tonight. Thank you for joining us.

ANCHOR #2:
Join us again tomorrow. And, have a pleasant evening.

VTR CLOSE: ANNC/MUS

GOOD AFTERNOON AMERICA

NEW ELEMENT

1. A more complex variety program with faster cues, camera breaks and VTR rolls.

PROPS/MATERIALS

1. VTR OPEN ANNC/MUS
2. VTR PACKAGE: Pikes Peak
3. :30 COMMERCIAL BREAK
4. VTR V/O SOT V/O: Fishing
5. 1:00 COMMERCIAL BREAK
6. VTR CLOSE

CONSIDERATIONS

1. This exercise requires you to put together all your skills for a complex program. This is a good time to review the helpful tips in Chapter 8.

2. Your hosts should not use a news desk. They should be seated in chairs or stools a la Good Morning America. You might use chairs and a coffee table.

3. You have some quick camera breaks as you move from the anchor position to the interview position with only two cameras. Plan your blocking and timing and it should work fine.

7. To plan your production without having to write in this book, loose scripts and forms are found in the *Multi-Camera Director Supplement.* If you don't have the *Supplement,* ask your instructor for forms, or create your own. Permission is given to photocopy any item found in the *Supplement.*

AIRDATE/TIME ________________

VTR OPEN:

ANNC/MUS
"Time now for Good Afternoon America."

MUSIC SWELL
TRANSITION TO STUDIO

HOST # 1:
Hello, I'm __________ and welcome to the show. This afternoon we continue with our travel series. Today we'll drive the highest road in the Rocky Mountains and catch the biggest fish in northern Manitoba.

HOST #2:

And I'm ________________. We start today with a look at a place to take your family on vacation this summer. One of the fastest growing recreation areas in the country—the Rocky Mountains. In Colorado alone, there are 52 peaks that reach 14,000 feet. One of them has a road to the top.

PACKAGE 1:00

HOST #2 AD LIBS REACTION

And we'll be back with more in our travel series when Good Afternoon America continues in a moment.

COMMERCIAL :30

HOST #1 -

In our next segment we travel to northern Manitoba, Canada, where the land is tundra, the fish are hungry and huge and the mosquitoes are vicious. Thousands of sports fishermen travel to Canada each year to fish the many lakes and rivers in northern Manitoba.

V/O SOT V/O

Here in northern Manitoba, the big draw is the Northern Pike, a fish that exceeds thirty pounds in these lakes.

SOUND UP ON FISHING SEQUENCE

V/O:

The fisherman you're seeing here is Barry Jones, well known in the fishing industry for his success in pursuing the Northern Pike.

HOST #2:
If you would like more information on the many fishing and hunting lodges in Canada, you can call the Canadian Tourism Hotline at 1-800-BIG-PIKE.

And we'll be back with more adventure after this message.

COMMERCIAL 1:00

INTERVIEW SEGMENT 2:00

HOST #2:
INTERVIEWS TRAVEL AGENT ABOUT ANOTHER LOCATION

CLOSE:

That's our show for today. Please tune in again tomorrow when our guests will include the winner of this year's Publishers Clearing House Sweepstakes.

CLOSE VTR/SOT:

MUS, ANNC, TITLE

Appendices

Pre-sets
① Tal H/S
② Easel
EFX = CG/color

R F EFX
R O ANNC MIC
R Q ANNC

AIRDATE/TIME ________________

F EFX

CG - "MORNING NEWS AND WEATHER WITH

______________________________"

O ANNC MIC

Q ANNC

R O TAL MIC
R Q TAL
R ≠ ①

ANNC:

You're watching ________________.
(Station Call Letters)
the leader in up-to-the-minute news coverage. Time now for the Morning News and Weather with

______________________________.
(Name)

O TAL MIC

Q TAL
≠ ①
Kill ANNC MIC

(DISSOLVE H/S TAL)

R ②

TAL:

Good morning. I'm ___________ and here are today's top stories. In local news, a man is behind bars tonight after a high speed police chase through the streets of the city. The man, who has not yet been identified, is suspected of having stolen more than 100 automobiles in the area over the past year. In national news, the President and First Lady left Washington today to vacation in Martha's Vineyard.

T ②

R ①

(EASEL PIC #1 - President/First Lady)

The President will be joined by the Vice President. Their vacation is expected to last ten days, although it could be cut short, according to a White House spokesperson. The

T ①

spokesperson told reporters today that the President may find it necessary to spend extra time lobbying legislators on his latest health care reform package.

① zm in slowly to CU

In international news, some Australians had a rude awakening this morning. A meteorite hit the township of Broken Hill in New South Wales last night, causing earthquake-like vibrations throughout the area. Hundreds of distressed residents called police saying they had seen a huge white light plummeting toward the ground. Police were not aware of the exact location of impact, but scientists confirmed it was a meteorite.

① zm slowly out to H/S

In sports, the Houston Rockets celebrate another NBA title as they beat the Orlando Magic in four straight games. This is the second national sports victory for the city of Houston and one that will not soon be forgotten.

Today's weather forecast looks fair and mild for the remainder of the day. Temperatures will drop to the mid 40s by midnight tonight. And tomorrow looks to be slightly cooler with a high of 68 degrees.

R ✗ EFX
R O ANNC MIC
R Q ANNC

The week-long outlook calls for a warming trend by the middle of the week, followed by a chance of increasing wind and showers as a minor front moves across the state. That's our up-date for this morning. Please tune in again for the Midday News for more top stories, sports and weather. I'm ______________, have a good morning.

✗ EFX

O ANNC MIC

Q ANNC

Kill TAL MIC

CG - "MORNING NEWS AND WEATHER WITH ______________________________"

ANNC:

This has been the Morning News with ______________________________.

And you have been watching ______________-TV, your choice for news and information.

R FSAPO

FSAPO

Pre-sets ① H/S TAL ② Print EFX = CG/VTR	AIRDATE/TIME ________________
R Roll VTR R ⊀ VTR SND UP R O ANNC MIC R Q ANNC	
Roll VTR	VTR SOT (THEME MUSIC)
⊀ VTR SND UP O ANNC MIC MUS UNDER Q ANNC	TITLE: CG/VTR "Top of the Morning with ________________."
R O TAL MIC R Q TAL R ⊀ ①	
O TAL MIC Q TAL ⊀ ①	ANNC: You're watching __________-TV. Time now for Top Of The Morning, with your host ______________________________.

① ZM OUT slowly to include print

HOST:

Hello, and welcome to Top of the Morning. Today, we've got some fun things in store for you. We've got some suggestions for what to do around town this weekend. We've got some weather updates. And, to start off, did you know about this weekend's benefit art auction at the Circle Gallery? I'd like to show you one of the prints by Bob Smith that will be up for auction.

R ②

T ②

R ① H/S TAL

TAL SHOWS PRINT

TAL AD LIBS A BRIEF

DESCRIPTION OF THE PRINT

T ①

VTR re-cue for close

Change EFX to CG/color CG page 2

They wouldn't give us the original. That's because the original is pretty valuable. This is a reproduction of "Stardust," one of only a few original works by the popular Bob Smith.

① zm out slowly to waist

Sixty percent of the proceeds from the sale will go to the Children's Hospital Oncology Fund. Bidding for Stardust will start at $5,000. You won't want to miss out on the chance to bid. For more information, call the Circle Gallery at 551-5151.

R ② on letter

Next, we have viewer mail, a regular segment on Top Of The Morning. Today's letter comes from Carolyn Jones of Bend, Oregon who writes:

T ②

CU EASEL PIC - LETTER

R ①

"Why do you continually promote the works of Canadian artist Bob Smith on your program? There are plenty of other artists of much greater talent than this fake. Why don't you feature sculptor Bob Jones of Bend, Oregon? Thank you sincerely, Carolyn Jones, Bend, Oregon."

T ①

R ② on tickets

We'll get our producers on it right away.

What to do this weekend besides visiting the Circle Gallery? It's time for the yearly Food Fest at Civic Center Park which opens Friday morning and runs all weekend. Admission is free, but you'll need to buy these.

T ②

R EFX

SHOW CU - TAL HOLDS TICKETS

Food tickets are available all around the park at the reasonable price of 5 for $10. These tickets are redeemable at any food concession. If you've never been to the Food Fest before, this is a good time to get out and see how much fun it is.

T EFX

R ①

CG - FOOD FEST INFO HOTLINE
555-FOOD

Call the Food Fest Hotline for a full list of restaurants and entertainment.

T ①

Change to:
CG P1
EFX= CG/VTR

Let's take a look at weather and see what the weekend has in store. The outlook for today is continued sunshine. More of the same tomorrow. Sunny and dry. And the weather experts tell us to expect the trend to continue for the rest of the week. Good news for Food Fest or for anything else you plan to do this weekend.

R ②

And finally, today—remember our elementary school poetry contest? Well we have the winning poem from this year's competition in the 2nd grade category. Before I read this, I just want you to get a look at it—we gave her extra points for her fabulous handwriting.

T ②

R ①

EASEL PIC - POEM

AD LIB ABOUT NEAT HANDWRITING

T ①

R ②

Her name is Lana Davis. She is only 9 years old and a 2nd grader at Skyline Elementary.
And here is her poem.

T ②

R ①	"If stars can be together in the sky Then why can't we stand side by side? If stars can twinkle so bright Then why can't we, instead of fight. Stars are peaceful and nice to see. That's what we should try to be."
T ①	
R Roll VTR R ⊄ VTR SND UP	Thank you, Lana, for your poem. You deserved to win and we look forward to seeing many more poems from you in the future.
Roll VTR	That's it for today. Thanks for joining me for Top Of The Morning. I'm your host, ___________________, wishing you a pleasant day.
⊄ VTR SND UP	
R O ANNC MIC R Q ANNC	
O ANNC MIC MUS UNDER Q ANNC	ANNC: You've been watching Top Of The Morning, with ___________________. Stay tuned for the Afternoon Report, here on _____________-TV, your best source for news, sports, and weather.
Kill TAL MIC	
R FSAPO	
FSAPO	

Pre-sets
EFX = CG/color
① 2 sht
② TAL #2 H/S

R Roll VTR
R F VTR SND UP

Roll VTR
F VTR
SND UP

VTR OPEN:

ANNC/MUS
"Time now for Good Afternoon America."

O TAL MICS
SWELL MUS

R F MUS
R Q TAL
R ✗ ①

MUSIC SWELL
TRANSITION TO STUDIO

F MUS
Q TAL
✗ ①

re-cue VTR

HOST # 1:
Hello, I'm __________ and welcome to the show. This afternoon we continue with our travel series. Today we'll drive the highest road in the Rocky Mountains and catch the biggest fish in northern Manitoba.

T ②

R R VTR
R VTR SND UP

HOST #2:

And I'm ______________. We start today with a look at a place to take your family on vacation this summer. One of the fastest growing recreation areas in the country—the Rocky Mountains. In Colorado alone, there are 52 peaks that reach 14,000 feet. One of them has a road to the top.

R VTR
T VTR SND UP
Kill MICS

R O MICS
R Q TAL
R (1)

O MICS
Q TAL
T (1)
RE-CUE VTR

PACKAGE 1:00

HOST #2 AD LIBS REACTION

R R VTR
R T VTR SND UP

Roll VTR
T VTR SND UP
Kill MICS

And we'll be back with more in our travel series when Good Afternoon America continues in a moment.

R O MICS
R Q TAL
R T (1)

COMMERCIAL :30

O MICS
Q TAL
T (1)
re-cue VTR

R Roll VTR R VTR MOS	HOST #1 - In our next segment we travel to northern Manitoba, Canada, where the land is tundra, the fish are hungry and huge and the mosquitoes are vicious. Thousands of sports fishermen travel to Canada each year to fish the many lakes and rivers in northern Manitoba.
Roll VTR T VTR MOS	
R TRACK UP VTR EFX = CG P2 / color	V/O SOT V/O Here in northern Manitoba, the big draw is the Northern Pike, a fish that exceeds thirty pounds in these lakes.
TRACK UP	
R Q TAL	SOUND UP ON FISHING SEQUENCE
TRACK DOWN Q TAL R ✗ EFX R RE-CUE VTR	V/O: The fisherman you're seeing here is Barry Jones, well known in the fishing industry for his success in pursuing the Northern Pike.
✗ EFX re-cue VTR	

R Roll VTR
R ✗ VTR SND UP

HOST #1:
If you would like more information on the many fishing and hunting lodges in Canada, you can call the Canadian Tourism Hotline at 1-800-BIG-PIKE.

Roll VTR
✗ VTR SND UP
Kill MICS
SET FOR INTERVIEW

And we'll be back with more adventure after this message.

R O MICS
R Q TAL
R ✗ (2)

COMMERCIAL 1:00

O MICS
Q TAL
✗ (2)
re-cue VTR

INTERVIEW SEGMENT 2:00

HOST #2:
INTERVIEWS TRAVEL AGENT ABOUT ANOTHER LOCATION

	HOST #2
② ZM OUT TO INCLUDE HOST 1	(THANK GUEST) That's our show for today. Please tune in again tomorrow when our guests will include the winner of this year's Publishers Clearing House Sweepstakes.
R Roll VTR R ≴ VTR SND UP	HOST #1: And our travel series continues as we visit the New England states with a special look at camping on the islands off the coast of Maine.
ROLL VTR	HOST #2: Thanks for joining us. Have a wonderful evening.
≴ VTR SND UP kill MICS	
R FSAPO	CLOSE VTR/SOT: MUS, ANNC, TITLE
FSAPO	

BIBLIOGRAPHY

Armer, Alan A. *Directing Television and Film.* Belmont, Cal: Wadsworth Publishing Co.

Carlson, Verne and Sylvia Carlson. *Professional Lighting Handbook.* Boston: Focal Press, 1985. Professional lighting methods and hardware.

Clifford, Martin. *Microphones.* 2nd ed. Blue Ridge Summit, Penn: TAB Books, 1982.

Cole, Toby, and Helen Krich Chinoy, eds. *Directors on Directing.* 2nd ed. New York: Bobbs-Merrill, 1979.

Compesi, Ronald J. and Ronald E. Sherriffs,. *Small Format Television Production.* 4th Edition. Boston: Allyn and Bacon, 1997.

Herlinger, Mark. *The Single-Camera Director* Western Media Products, 1997.

Hickman, Harold. *Television Directing.* New York, NY: McGraw-Hill College, 1991.

Hyde, Stuart W. *Television & Radio Announcing.* Boston, MA: Houghton Mifflin, 1998.

Lukas, Christopher. *Directing for Film and Television.* Garden City, NY: Anchor Press/Doubleday, 1985.

Millerson, Gerald. *The Technique of Lighting for Television and Motion Pictures.* Woburn: Focal Press, 1982.

Nisbett, Alec. *The Use of Microphones.* 2nd ed. Woburn, Mass: Focal Press, 1983.

Quick, John, and Herbert. Wolff, *Small Studio Videotape Recording.* 3rd Reading, Mass.: Addison-Wesley, 1980.

Watts, Harris. *Directing On Camera.* Woburn, MA: Focal Press, 1997.

Zettl, Herbert. *Television Production Handbook.* 7th Belmont, Cal.: Wadsworth Publishing Co.,1998.